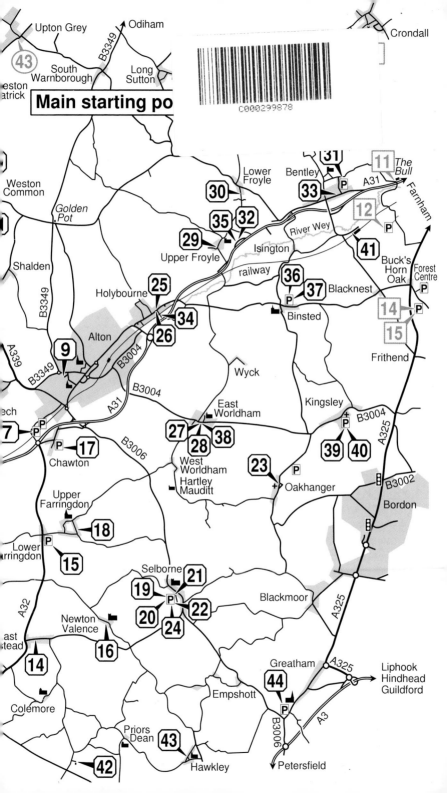

Main starting po[int]

1 Wield and Preston Candover

About 10 km/6¼ miles with a short cut of 2km/1¼ miles; rolling farmland on the chalk. OS maps 1:25000 144 Basingstoke; 1:50000 185 Winchester.

Start from Upper Wield, parking near the church, SU 629 387, or from Preston Candover, parking in the layby opposite the school, SU 607 418.

Linking walks 2❋ 3✿ 4☆ (32)❋ (33)❦ (37)❖

The Purefoy Arms ☎ 01256 389777
The Yew Tree ☎ 01256 389224

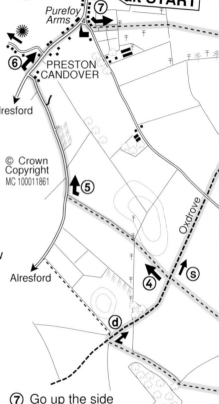

© Crown Copyright MC 100011861

From Wield Church go out to the main village street and turn L.

① Walk along the road past the pond as far as the L bend (300m) then ahead on the drive (100m).

② Just before the drive bends R, climb into the field L. Follow the hedge R through the fields, down to the corner (500m), over the rise and down to the end of the next field (500m) then L along the bottom edge to the road (250m).

③ Go L up the road and into the corner of the R field (100m). Follow the path out of the corner on the bisecting line, through the dip and up to the far hedge, 200m R of a little wood (700m). Go through the hedge. ➔④ ahead or ➔⑤ turn R

⑤ *Short cut of 2 km/1¼ miles missing Preston Candover & pub: Follow the Oxdrove track over the road (600m), ahead over the rise (800m), down past a thicket R and over the next field into the corner with the trees (600m).* ❖ ➔⑨

④ Cross the next field slightly R to the highest electricity pole in the hedge (350m). Carry on at the R edge of the next field down to the road (550m).

⑤ Walk down the road R to Preston Candover (800m). ❋

⑥ Turn R along the village street to the **Purefoy Arms** (500m). ❦

⑦ Go up the side road next to the church (100m) and turn L on the path after the houses. Pass between paddocks (200m) and go straight up the middle of the large field. Aim 50m R of the top corner (300m). In the next field aim for the highest part of the top hedge (700m).

⑧ Cross the hedge and turn L beside it, over the rise and down to the corner with trees (350m). ❖

2

⑨ Turn R up beside the trees. Keep to the winding L edge of the same field until over the top and ahead into the next field (650m). ❉ Cross to the R corner of the wood ═ (350m) and go on beside it into the narrow corner (300m). Enter the wood and turn R immediately to the next field (70m).

⑪ Pass through the trees (40m), over a track and ahead beside a garden (100m). Bear L over two narrow fields and go L between hedges to Lower Wield (200m). ✿

⑫ Follow the road R to the 90° bend (300m). Turn L on the track (15m) & R through the trees, soon beside a garden. Over the brow of the hill, slightly R, descend beside the fence to the road (300m). ☆ (The **Yew Tree** is 100m R.)

⑬ Continue in the field opposite along the R hedge (600m). Cross the next field slightly L to the trees at the L end of the hedge opposite (300m). Carry on between fields past the village hall (150m) and along the R edge of the village green into Upper Wield (150m).

ⓐ *Another time start along the little fields behind the church to the road R (400m).*

ⓑ *Follow the road L to the drive at Wield Wood Lodge (400m).*

ⓒ *At the gate after the drive (30m) turn L into the garden. Cross the L end of the garden to the paddocks (30m) then follow the stiles ½R to the bottom end of the high hedge (250m). Cross the next field obliquely L to the wood (500m). Go on through the next field, along the R hedge and ahead to the top, at a slight bend in the hedge (500m).*

ⓓ *On the track outside go R into the dip and up onto the next ridge. Watch out for a cross path (600m).*

↠④ *in field L or* ↠⑤ *ahead*

⑩ Make for the top L corner. Go on through the belt of trees and over the track into the next field (250m). Cut across the top corner to a projecting hedge bend (150m) and continue along the L hedge to the corner at the trees (150m).

1 mile

1 km

N
W — E
S

LOWER WIELD

UPPER WIELD

The Yew Tree

chalkpit

ield Wood Farm

VH

START

⑧ ⑨ ⑩ ⑪ ⑫ ⑬ ① ② ③ ⓐ ⓑ ⓒ

2 Lower Wield and Bradley

About 6½ km/4 miles with an extension of 2¾ km/1¾ miles, via Woodland Trust Home Farm at Burkham, and an extension of 1¼ km/¾ mile; undulating chalk farmland. OS maps 1:25000 144 Basingstoke, 1:50000 175 Winchester.

There is no large parking place. Start from Bradley Church, SU 635 417. On the extended version there is a Woodlands Trust car park at Burkham, SU 654 415. There is a roadside parking spot at Lower Wield Farm, SU 636 404.

Linking walks 1❋ 2✸ 4✧ (33)❄ (37)✪ ***The Yew Tree*** 01256 389224

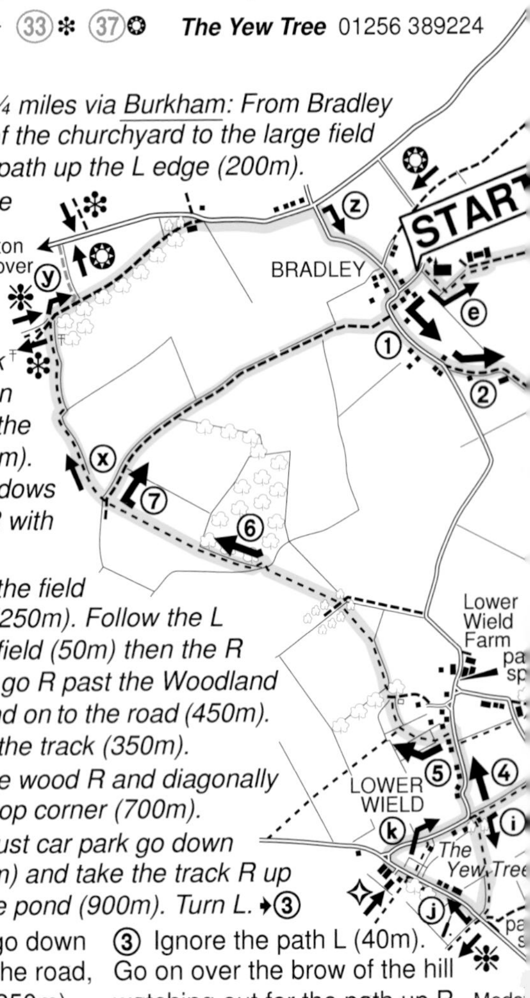

(e) Extension of 2¾ km/1¾ miles via Burkham: From Bradley Church cross the bottom of the churchyard to the large field beyond (80m). Follow the path up the L edge (200m). After the barns L, follow the track (450m).
The right of way continues R of the hedge but it is easier to use the track L of it and cross back at the end (400m). Keep on to the corner and through the trees to the next field (300m). (The Woodland Trust meadows (Home Farm) are on the R with many paths across them.)

(f) Bear slightly R across the field to exit at the far R corner (250m). Follow the L fence ahead into the next field (50m) then the R fence (200m). At the track go R past the Woodland Trust side track (100m), and on to the road (450m). Cross and continue down the track (350m).

(g) Go round the end of the wood R and diagonally up the meadow to the far top corner (700m).

(h) From the Woodland Trust car park go down the road to the bend (100m) and take the track R up to the 4-way junction at the pond (900m). Turn L. ➜(3)

(1) From Bradley Church go down the lane (100m) and L on the road, to the edge of the village (350m).

(2) Bear L on the track next to the thatched cottage (150m). Carry on at the R edge of the fields (950m) and ahead up through the wood to the 4-way junction at the pond (350m). Take the onward track. ✸

(3) Ignore the path L (40m). Go on over the brow of the hill watching out for the path up R (250m). Climb to the field and follow the L hedge away from the track (200m). Stay ahead over the fields (700m), along the track L of the hedge (200m), over a road and on to Lower Wield (300m). Turn R.

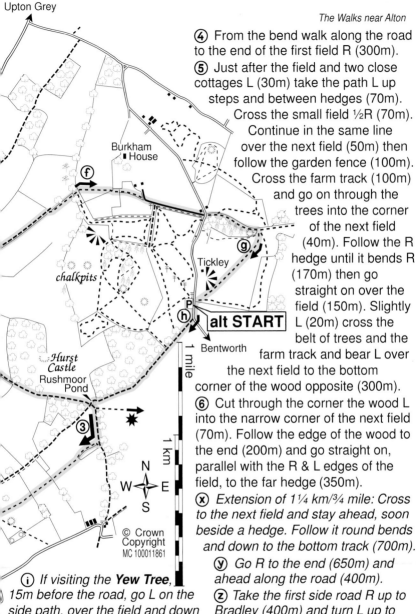

Upton Grey

Burkham House

chalkpits

Tickley

Hurst Castle

Rushmoor Pond

Bentworth

N W E S

1 mile

1 km

© Crown Copyright MC 100011861

alt START

④ From the bend walk along the road to the end of the first field R (300m).

⑤ Just after the field and two close cottages L (30m) take the path L up steps and between hedges (70m). Cross the small field ½R (70m). Continue in the same line over the next field (50m) then follow the garden fence (100m). Cross the farm track (100m) and go on through the trees into the corner of the next field (40m). Follow the R hedge until it bends R (170m) then go straight on over the field (150m). Slightly L (20m) cross the belt of trees and the farm track and bear L over the next field to the bottom corner of the wood opposite (300m).

⑥ Cut through the corner the wood L into the narrow corner of the next field (70m). Follow the edge of the wood to the end (200m) and go straight on, parallel with the R & L edges of the field, to the far hedge (350m).

ⓧ *Extension of 1¼ km/¾ mile: Cross to the next field and stay ahead, soon beside a hedge. Follow it round bends and down to the bottom track (700m).*

ⓨ *Go R to the end (650m) and ahead along the road (400m).*

ⓩ *Take the first side road R up to Bradley (400m) and turn L up to the church (100m).*

⑦ Turn R and follow the hedge through several large fields over the hill (1000m). Stay on the same track down to the road at Bradley (250m). Go L on the road round the bends (100m) and up the lane to the church (100m).

ⓘ *If visiting the **Yew Tree**, 15m before the road, go L on the side path, over the field and down the fence to the road R (350m). ❖*

ⓙ *Turn R up to the pub (150m). Continue up the road (200m).*

ⓚ *After the next house L, at the drives on the brow of the hill, take the path R across the fields to the next road (150m). Go R on the road (150m) and round the bend.*

5

3 Bentworth and Lower Wield

About 8½ km/5¼ miles over undulating farmland on the chalk; a bluebell wood; lots of stiles. OS maps 1:25000 144 Basingstoke, 1:50000 185 Winchester.

There is no large parking place. Start from Bentworth Church, SU 665 402, or at Lower Wield Farm, parking beside the road, SU 636 404.

The Star ☎ 01420 561224   Linking walks 1✿ 2✹ 4✹ 5❖ 6✿ 8✹
The Yew Tree ☎ 01256 389224
The Sun ☎ 01420 562338

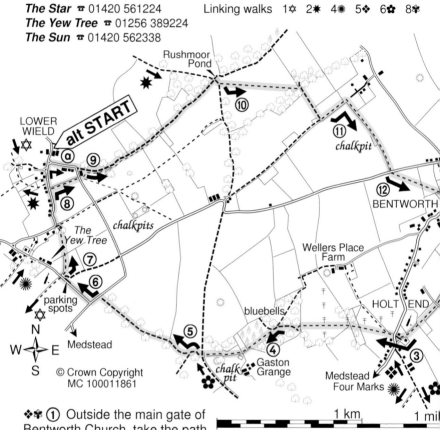

❖✹ ① Outside the main gate of Bentworth Church, take the path between the churchyard & garden and over the next road (200m). Go on between gardens and down the L edge of the field (300m).

② At the bottom turn R on the path up the edge of the next field. Stay ahead at the R edge of the fields, over the sunken track (Tinkers Lane) (300m), over the drive of Bentworth Hall (350m), past the cricket field and between gardens to the road at Holt End (400m). ✹✿

③ Cross the road slightly R, into the field opposite (50m). Follow the hedge to the slight bend (40m) then diverge a bit over the field towards the trees and small power lines (250m). Pass through a plantation into the corner of the next large field. Cross it, diverging from the L edge to the gate at the wood (350m). Carry on ahead through the wood and join the track converging from R (150m).

6

④ Keep on (L), disregarding side tracks, to the end of the wood (250m), along the L fence across a narrow field with Gaston Grange L (40m), past the chalkpit with trees (150m) and down to the track junction in the valley (100m).

⑤ Cross the straight track and follow the curving track opposite round to the fork (70m). Take the R track up to the next road (800m).

⑥ Turn L along the road (100m) and R along the side road to the path crossing from the end of the L field (300m). ✿ (The **Yew Tree** is 100m ahead.)

⑦ Take the path in the R field up round the fence and through the trees R of the houses above (300m). Join the road at the bend (15m L) and follow it R to the second group of houses L (300m). ✳

Sun Inn

②

y's Lane

ⓐ *Slightly longer alternative: If you like looking at houses, walk on through Lower* Wield *(200m)*

and turn R on the side road (200m). Don't go round the next bend but continue on the path ahead. ➔⑨

⑧ Take the path R along the end of the field (200m). Cross the lane and pass R of the barn (50m).

⑨ Join the path at the edge of the R field. At the chalk pit rejoin the track (150m) then continue in the field. When the field path ends, join the track under the trees and carry on to the 4-way track junction at Rushmoor Pond (900m).

⑩ Take the R track to the R bend (40m) then the footpath L over the field diagonally to the far L corner (600m). Join the track outside and descend R through the belt of trees then between fields (250m).

⑪ At the bottom go L to the farm gate (250m) then R up the edge of the fields to the next road (550m).

⑫ Cross to the field opposite and aim obliquely for the hedge corner top L near houses (400m). Cross the next small field in the same line to emerge on the green opposite the **Star Inn** (70m). The church is down the road L.

The whole route of this walk lies on the chalk with its characteristic rolling landscape. Chalk seems to be associated in the English mind with the southern downs and the white cliffs of Dover but it stretches westwards to Devon and up through East Anglia to Yorkshire where the Wolds are the rolling country. It probably covered the rest of Britain with mountains protruding. A small outlier survives in Northern Ireland preserved under basalt. The same chalk mass extends into Northern France which made soft digging for the Channel Tunnel. From Weald to Wolds the chalk is concealed by a mantle of boulder clay, detritus of glaciation, which determines the type of soil.

outcrop of the chalk

4 Medstead and Upper Wield

About 10 km/6¼ miles with extensions of 1 km/¾ mile and ½ km; undulating farmland; lots of stiles. OS 1:25000 132 or 144, 1:50000 185 Winchester.

Start from the car park at Medstead village green, SU 658 369. There are a few roadside parking spots in Upper Wield and near Lower Wield Farm.

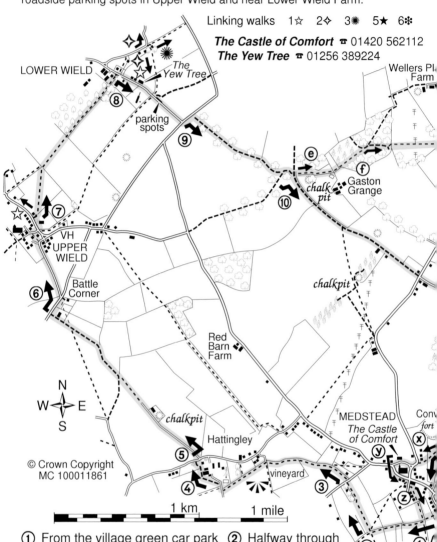

Linking walks 1☆ 2✧ 3✻ 5★ 6❈

The Castle of Comfort ☎ 01420 562112
The Yew Tree ☎ 01256 389224

© Crown Copyright
MC 100011861

① From the village green car park at Medstead cross the football pitch (100m) to take the path between the last two houses (120m). Enter the L field but carry on in the same direction at the R hedge and cross the ends of narrow fields (300m).

② Halfway through the next wide field (100m) turn R on the cross path. Disregard the oblique path R (to the village centre) and keep to the middle of the field then ahead beside a hedge (400m).

8

③ Cross the road into the corner of the field opposite (20m) and carry on at the R edge all the way to Hattingley (600m). Disregard concrete track R after the vineyard and keep on at the edge of the field behind the houses (400m).

④ Turn R on the next farm track (30m). After the gateway bear L on the side track which skirts L of the farm buildings to the road (250m).

⑤ Slightly R (40m), opposite the house, take the concrete track L.

Stay ahead to the end of the field (800m) and along the track with R & L bends to the next road (750m).

⑥ Turn R (120m) and fork L on the road to Upper Wield (400m). At the bend pass between the houses ahead and go along the lane to see the church (150m). ☆

Return to the main road (100m) and turn L (80m).

⑦ At the track after the pond turn R to the field and cross to the diagonal corner (400m). Go straight over the next field to the R edge of the wood and on to the road in Lower Wield (800m). ✧✷

⑧ Walk down past the ***Yew Tree*** (300m) to the T-junction (350m).

⑨ Start along the road L (100m) then turn off on the track R under trees. When it meets another track (800m) carry on (L) round to the end at the straight track (70m).

ⓔ Extension of 1 km/¾ mile: In the field opposite, follow the R fence up past the chalkpit and past Gaston Grange to the wood (300m). Stay ahead through the trees. Soon after the track from the fields L is a track fork (250m).

ⓕ Fork R to the edge of the wood. At the field R, bear L into the field ahead (150m). Cross to the far R corner (350m). Go on through the plantation then the next field to the far L corner near houses (300m). ★

ⓖ Go R on the road R (100m) and L along the farm track (300m). ❄

ⓗ Turn off at the start of the 2nd field R and follow the edge to the other end (700m). Go round the corner and on along the edge of the field (200m) then cross the road to the shared drive. ➧⑪

⑩ Follow the track R to the road (1200m). Cross and go along the side road opposite which curves L & R to a shared drive R (400m).

⑪ Take the drive between houses (350m). Continue through the field (200m), slightly R over the middle of the next (200m) and along the R edge of the next (300m). Pass out at the Convent of St Lucy and turn R into the adjacent field. (The little path R leads to the fort).

ⓧ Extension of 500m/¼ mile into Medstead: Take the oblique path L across the field then between gardens to the road (250m).

*ⓨ Slightly L, take the side road R round past the **Castle of Comfort** to the main road (200m) then turn back L past Medstead Church to the crossroads (150m).*

ⓩ Go along Green Stile R (70m). Turn into the track before the first house L and take the path behind the houses (250m). Turn L on the cross path to the car park (200m).

⑫ Go into the field ½L a little way (50m) then, at the projecting hedge corner, join the convent drive and walk out to the road (250m). Turn L to the car park (150m).

5 Bentworth, Thedden and Wivelrod

About 9 km/5½ miles with a short cut of 2 km/1¼ miles; undulating farmland on the chalk. OS maps 1:25000 144 Basingstoke, 1:50000 175 Winchester.

There is no large parking place. Start from Bentworth Church, SU 665 402, or the adjacent village hall.

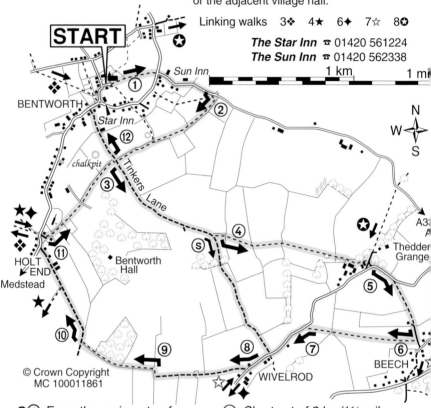

Linking walks 3❖ 4★ 6✦ 7☆ 8✪

The Star Inn ☎ 01420 561224
The Sun Inn ☎ 01420 562338

✪① From the main gate of Bentworth Church go through the churchyard, R of the church, and on along the footpath to the road (300m). Walk down the side road opposite, round bends, to the **Sun** (200m) and on (250m).

② Just before the next road junction enter the field R and follow the bottom edges up the valley to the sunken Tinkers Lane which is a track between fields (800m).

③ Turn L. Stay on Tinkers' Lane over the hill and down across the next valley to the bend (900m).

ⓢ *Short cut of 2 km/1¼ miles: Continue between the fields on Tinkers Lane round the bend and up to the road (900m). Turn R.* ✦⑧

④ Turn off L on the footpath ahead up beside the hedge (120m). Cross the next field slightly R up through the middle (150m) and go straight over the next to the highest point (200m). Keep on over the next field descending towards the R end of the hedge (400m). Pass through and keep on beside the perimeter fence of Thedden Farm (80m). When level with the buildings don't

10

continue round the field. Go through the trees to the barns (100m), round L to the track (50m) and R,L to the road (40m).

⑤ Walk L down the road (200m). On the slight L bend watch out for the path R up the edge of the field. Follow it to the house (350m) and continue down the track towards the houses of Beech (100m). ☆

⑥ Before reaching the road turn into the field R and go straight up the middle. From the bend in the top boundary (600m) cross the next field on the same line (ie slightly L) to the road (200m).

⑦ Walk along the road L past the end of Tinkers Lane (300m). ✦

⑧ Keep on ahead to the houses of Wivelrod (200m) then branch R down the track after Maple Cottage. Stay on the track across the valley and up to the end (600m).

⑨ A little way R along the top edge of the field (50m), turn L into the corner of the adjacent field. Follow the L edge over the field, down through the edge of the wood and up to the next track (500m).

⑩ Walk along the track R, round the L bend ★ and all the way to the road at Holt End (750m). ❖

⑪ Go R on the road briefly then cut across the grass R to the garden gates (100m) and go on between the gardens. Continue ahead outside the cricket field and in the same line over the fields (350m). Cross the tarmac drive of Bentworth Hall and continue along L hedges to the track (Tinkers Lane) (400m).

⑫ Walk up Tinkers Lane L to the road (400m). Turn R to the road junction near the **Star Inn** (80m) and L to the church (100m).

Galls on oak drawn actual size.

Galls are outgrowths on plants induced by other organisms. The ones shown are all caused by small insects of the wasp group when they lay eggs - in these cases unfertilized. The outgrowths provide homes and food for the parthenogenic larvae. The adults that emerge mate and lay fertilized eggs that form galls elsewhere on oaks.

The artichoke or hop gall forms from a bud and is caused by *Andricus fecundata*. It supports a single larva for two years. The fertilized eggs are laid on oak catkins and form hairy galls. The silk button (spangle) galls of *Neuroterus numismalis* under the apex of the leaf also house single larvae. Their other generation causes blister galls on oak leaves in spring. The common spangle galls - under leaf bases - house *N. quercusbaccarum* larvae. The galls of their other generation look like red currants on oak catkins.

Spangle galls look like surface bumps but are stalked discs. They are picked off and eaten like biscuits by dormice and fall off before the leaves in autumn, sometimes in vast numbers.

The Natural History of the Oak Tree R Lewington & D Streeter 1993 Dorling Kindersley

6 Medstead, Gaston Grange and Wivelrod

About 10 km/6¼ miles with a short cut of 2 km/1¼ miles; undulating farmland and woods; bluebells in season. OS maps 1:25000 144 Basingstoke or 132 Winchester, 1:50000 186 Aldershot or 185 Winchester.

Start from the roadside at Medstead Church, SU 654 371. There is a car park at the football ground at the south edge of the village, SU 658 369. Chawton Park Wood car park, SU 672 360, can be used with an extension of 2 km/1¼ mile.

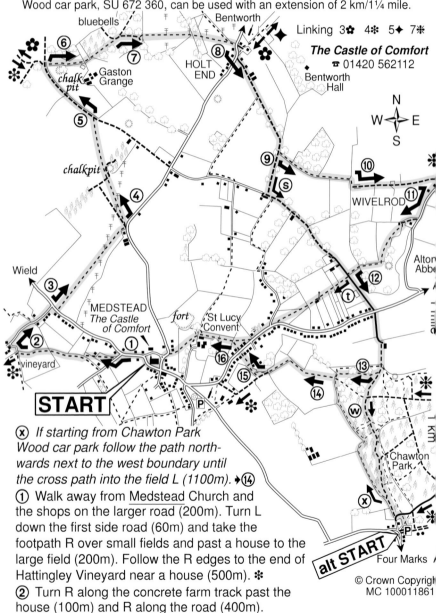

Linking 3✿ 4❄ 5✦ 7❈

The Castle of Comfort
☎ 01420 562112

(x) *If starting from Chawton Park Wood car park follow the path north-wards next to the west boundary until the cross path into the field L (1100m).* ➤⑭

① Walk away from <u>Medstead</u> Church and the shops on the larger road (200m). Turn L down the first side road (60m) and take the footpath R over small fields and past a house to the large field (200m). Follow the R edges to the end of Hattingley Vineyard near a house (500m). ❈

② Turn R along the concrete farm track past the house (100m) and R along the road (400m).

③ At the T-junction, turn R (30m) then cross to the field opposite. Go straight down aiming for the distant house at the bottom. Pass L of the house almost to the road (700m).

④ Turn L across the same field. The public footpath follows the slight valley across to the chalkpit trees but it is easier to follow the farm track across the field (400m) then R (100m). After the chalkpit follow the path along the valley to the edge of the field (400m).

⑤ Walk L along the track between the fields to the side track L on the R bend in the trees (500m). ✿

⑥ Opposite the side track enter the R field. Follow the R fence up past a chalkpit with trees and on past Gaston Grange R into the wood (350m). Soon after a side track L is a fork in the track (250m).

⑦ Fork R to the edge of the wood. At the field R, bear L into the field ahead (150m). Cross to the far R corner (350m). Go though the trees then over the next field to the far L corner near a house (300m). ✦

⑧ Turn R on the road (100m) and L on the farm track (100m). After houses and barns keep on to the bend (650m) and round it (100m).

Ⓢ *Short cut of 2km/1¼ miles: Stay on the track to its end (300m). Go L on the track from the road into the dip and up past a house (600m) to the path R between fields (200m).*

Ⓣ *Follow this path in a straight line to the next road (600m). Turn R on the road to the corner of a field between gardens (200m) and bear R on the footpath (120m). ➤⑯*

⑨ Enter the end of the L field. Go down the R edge, up through the wood and over a field (500m).

⑩ In the next field turn R to the corner (50m) and join the track between the fields. Follow it down L into the valley and up to the road at Wivelrod (600m). ✳

⑪ Walk R past the farm buildings along the road (300m). Turn down the track R before the next solitary house R (100m) and L into the field. Go down round the trees L to the bottom of the valley (300m), into the next field and up the R edge. Carry on across the end of the next field to the vehicle track (250m).

⑫ Turn L along the track (300m). Continue ahead over the road. When the track bends to a house (200m) take the path ahead into Chawton Park Wood (200m).

Ⓦ *If going to Chawton Park car park, keep to paths ahead (900m).*

⑬ In the wood (40m) take the 2nd path R down to the field (350m).

⑭ Go straight over to a projecting hedge corner and on beside the hedge to the end (300m). Cross the end boundary and walk L through the narrow area of rough ground out to a track (300m). ✳ (For the village green/football car park stay ahead (450m).)

⑮ Don't go along the track but take the path R beside gardens to the road (250m). Continue between houses opposite (100m).

⑯ Cross the end of the next field. Keep on ahead to the end of the Convent buildings (250m) where a path joins from R. Continue into the field ahead (a small path R leads to the fort). Cross the field obliquely and pass out between gardens to the road (250m). The church is L (100m). Go through the churchyard to the parking place.

7 Chawton Park Wood, Wivelrod and Beech

About 9 km/5¾ miles with a 1 km/¾ mile woodland extension; undulating; best at bluebell time. OS maps 1:25000 132+144, 1:50000 186 Aldershot.

Start from the western car park of the field at Alton Sports Centre, SU 702 377, or, on the extension, from Chawton Park Wood car park, SU 672 360.

Linking walks 5☆ 6✳ 17✿

The French Horn
☎ 01420 83269
The Windmill
☎ 01420 563554
WIVELROD

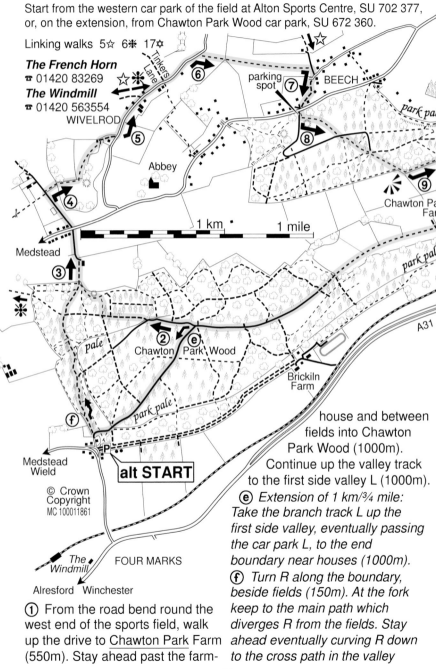

1 km   1 mile

alt START

© Crown
Copyright
MC 100011861

The Windmill   FOUR MARKS
Alresford   Winchester

house and between fields into Chawton Park Wood (1000m). Continue up the valley track to the first side valley L (1000m).

ⓔ *Extension of 1 km/¾ mile: Take the branch track L up the first side valley, eventually passing the car park L, to the end boundary near houses (1000m).*
ⓕ *Turn R along the boundary, beside fields (150m). At the fork keep to the main path which diverges R from the fields. Stay ahead eventually curving R down to the cross path in the valley*

① From the road bend round the west end of the sports field, walk up the drive to Chawton Park Farm (550m). Stay ahead past the farm-

14

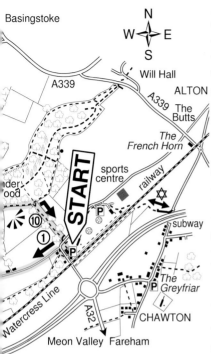

Basingstoke

N
W E
S

A339

Will Hall

A339

ALTON

The Butts

The French Horn

sports centre

railway

START

P

subway

P

The Greyfriar

CHAWTON

A32

Meon Valley Fareham

Watercress Line

at Wivelrod (300m). Continue on the road past the end of another track L (Tinkers Lane) (150m) and the next house R (150m) then watch out for a footpath R (150m).

⑥ Cross the field obliquely L to the bend in the opposite hedge (200m) and go down the middle of the next field to the track near the houses of Beech (750m).

⑦ Turn R to the lane (50m) and R along it. Keep on down the winding track to the valley road (250m). Cross and go up the track (70m).

⑧ Take the first side path L obliquely up the hillside to the forestry hard track (300m). Cross obliquely and keep on to the 5-way junction of tracks (250m). Continue ahead on the rising R path to the top edge of the wood (200m).

⑨ Join the converging boundary path and carry on (L) keeping to the edge of the wood, past a belt of trees R between fields (500m) to the end of the next field (250m).

⑩ In the next belt of trees take the path down R to the road (300m). Go up through the hedge opposite to the car park (100m).

(700m). ✳ *Go up the other side to the edge of the wood (250m).* ➥③

② Stay on the track ahead in the main valley, past a 2nd side valley (350m), to the next side track L (300m). ✳ Opposite it, climb to the top of the wood R (150m). Turn L along the edge to the cross path between the fields (150m). Turn R.

③ Stay ahead between the fields (200m), along the track to the road at the edge of Medstead (250m) and along the track opposite to the end of the R field (300m).

④ Take the path R along the edge and ahead R of the hedge in the next field (300m). At the bottom turn into the L field. Go up round the trees R and cross L to the track up from the shed (300m). Ascend, L of the house, to the road (100m).

⑤ Walk along the road L past the houses and the converging track ☆

The **Watercress Line** took this name when the Mid-Hants Railway Preservation Society purchased it from British Rail, track dismantling having already begun. Shares in the Society were issued in 1975. Trains started running from Alresford to Ropley in 1977 and the track was re-layed back to Alton in 1985. The original line was laid by the Alton, Alresford & Winchester Railway Co under an Act of 1860 and opened in 1865 when London trains went via Guildford. It was run by the LSWRCo which bought it in 1876. It had stations at Itchen Abass, Ropley & Medstead. The last British Rail train ran in 1973.

8 Bentworth to Warren Farm (and Lasham)

About 7½ km/4½ miles. This walk involves a ¾ mile stretch of the A339 which is not very busy mid-week and is avoided if the walk is linked to Walk 9.
An extension to Lasham of 4¼ km/2¾ miles also uses road but a quiet country lane. OS maps 1:25000 144 Basingstoke, 1:50000 186 Aldershot.

There is no large parking place. Start from Bentworth Church, SU 665 402.
On the extension there is parking near the churches in Lasham and Shalden.

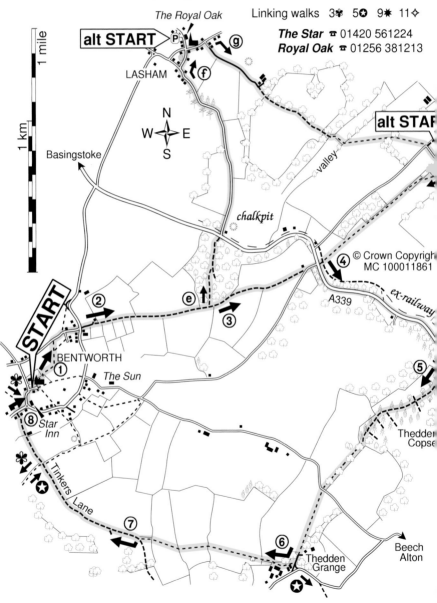

Linking walks 3❋ 5✿ 9❋ 11◇

The Star ☎ 01420 561224
Royal Oak ☎ 01256 381213

© Crown Copyright MC 100011861

① From the main gate take the path L of <u>Bentworth</u> Church (50m). In the field cross obliquely to the road but around the R side of the pit (250m). Turn R along the road to the T-junction (200m).

② Carry on down the cart track opposite, soon between fields, then up past a wood L (900m).

ⓔ *Extension of 4¾ km/2¼ miles to Lasham: In the wood take the path L down to the main road (500m). Walk up the road opposite, all the way to <u>Lasham</u> (1200m).*

ⓕ *At the first road junction follow the larger road R past the village pond to the crossroads near the church and **Royal Oak** (150m). Turn R on the Froyle road (150m).*

ⓖ *Opposite Church Farm Place take the farm track R, past houses, down into the valley and up past the farm buildings (500m). Keep on ahead until the track ends at a field on the side of a small valley (600m). Carry on at the edge into the next field (30m) and go R down the edge to the bottom of the valley (80m). Just round the corner cross the belt of trees and go up the other side ½L. Over the brow aim 80m L of the jutting corner with trees (300m). In the next field stay on the same oblique line down to the road (250m). Go up the road to the L bend in <u>Shalden</u> (200m).* ✧✽

ⓗ *Turn R to the church. Cross the churchyard ahead to the next field (120m). Go round the corner R (20m) and on along the edge (100m) then into the small field R. Cross to the far R corner (100m) then keep on along the R edge of the large field to the end of the*

wood (350m). Stay ahead down to the trees. Go on through the trees, over the farm track on the route of the <u>Basingstoke- Alton</u> railway to the main road (450m). Turn L. ➔④

③ Stay ahead down to the lane (700m) and the main road, A339 (120m). Turn R.

④ Follow the main road all the way to the field L after the houses at Warren Farm (1200m).

⑤ Two tracks enter the trees R. Take the L one up through the conifer plantation of Thedden Copse (800m). Cross the next field slightly L and go up beside the grounds of <u>Thedden</u> Grange into the trees (600m). ❍

⑥ Just before the road turn R on the path near the sheds. Follow it through the trees outside Thedden Farm and into the field (150m). Keep on along the L edge of the large field and through the hedge at the corner (80m). Go straight up the next field (400m), over two more (400m) then down beside the hedge to the wide cart track, Tinkers Lane (120m).

⑦ Continue (R) on Tinkers Lane up between the fields, down across a dry valley ✽ and up to the road in Bentworth (1200m).

⑧ Turn R to the ***Star Inn*** (100m) then L to the church (100m).

Chalkpits are scattered over the fields throughout the area. After a century or more of disuse many have become hidden in the circular clumps of trees which dot the hillsides. Chalk was spread on the less fertile clay soils and roasted in lime kilns to make quicklime for mortar. Some of the pits on the clay cap were for brick clay or wells.

9 Alton and Shalden

About 8½ km/5¼ miles with a ¾ mile stretch of A339 - less busy mid-week and avoided if linking to Walk 8. An extension of 3½ km/2¼ miles via Lasham and a short cut of 600m. OS maps 1:25000 144 Basingstoke, 1:50000 186 Aldershot.

Start in Alton; park at the bottom of Queens Road, SU 712 392, or walk in from the town centre. There is parking near the churches in Shalden and Lasham.

Linking walks   8✳   11❄

The Royal Oak ☎ 01256 381213

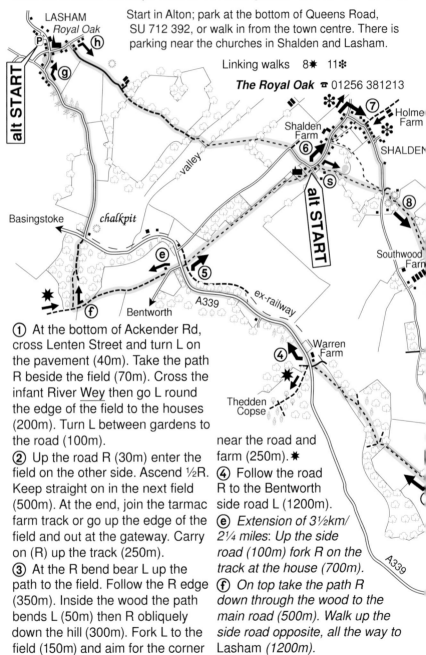

① At the bottom of Ackender Rd, cross Lenten Street and turn L on the pavement (40m). Take the path R beside the field (70m). Cross the infant River Wey then go L round the edge of the field to the houses (200m). Turn L between gardens to the road (100m).

② Up the road R (30m) enter the field on the other side. Ascend ½R. Keep straight on in the next field (500m). At the end, join the tarmac farm track or go up the edge of the field and out at the gateway. Carry on (R) up the track (250m).

③ At the R bend bear L up the path to the field. Follow the R edge (350m). Inside the wood the path bends L (50m) then R obliquely down the hill (300m). Fork L to the field (150m) and aim for the corner near the road and farm (250m). ✳

④ Follow the road R to the Bentworth side road L (1200m).

ⓔ *Extension of 3½km/ 2¼ miles: Up the side road (100m) fork R on the track at the house (700m).*

ⓕ *On top take the path R down through the wood to the main road (500m). Walk up the side road opposite, all the way to Lasham (1200m).*

ⓖ At the first road junction follow the larger road round R past the village pond to the crossroads, church and ***Royal Oak*** *(150m). Turn R on the Froyle road (150m)*

ⓗ Opposite Church Farm Place take the farm track R down into the valley and up past the farm buildings (500m). Keep on ahead until the track ends at a field on the side of a small valley (600m). Carry on into the next field (30m) then turn R down the edge to the bottom of the valley (80m). Just round the corner cross the belt of trees and go ½L up the other side. Over the brow aim 80m L of the jutting corner with trees (300m). In the next field stay on the same oblique line down to the road (250m). Walk up the road and round the L bend to the exit from the church (200m). ➔⑥

⑤ Opposite the side road climb the stepped path up the R bank. Go through the trees, over the ex-Basingstoke-Alton railway, and straight on up the field to pass R of the trees above.

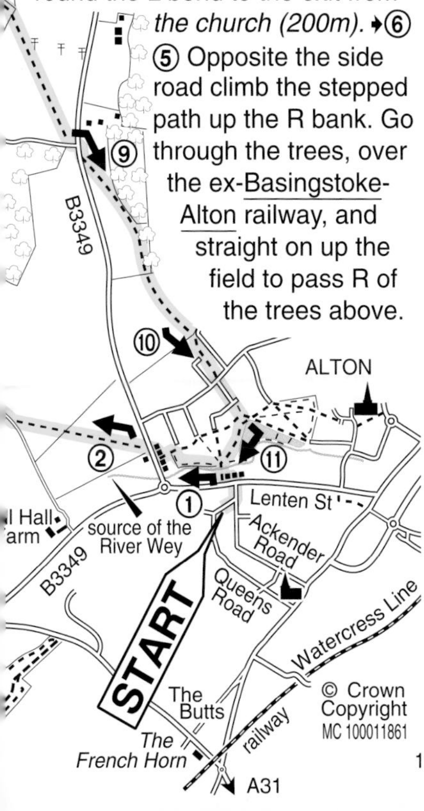

ALTON
⑨
⑩
②
⑪
①
B3349
B3349
Lenten St
Ackender Road
Queens Road
source of the River Wey
l Hall
arm
Watercress Line
START
The Butts
The French Horn
railway
A31

© Crown Copyright MC 100011861

Keep on beside the wood then at the L edge of the field (800m). At the corner go on into the next small field (100m). Exit R to the large field then follow the L edge (100m). Just round the corner (20m) enter the churchyard. Go through to the road in Shalden (120m).

ⓢ Short cut of 500m/½ mile: Up the road (40m), after the first garden, take the narrow path R down to the field (150m). Go on down ½R to the bottom of the valley then up the other side to the road near the wood R (300m). Cross to the path opposite. ➔⑧

⑥ Walk up the road through Shalden (450m). ❇

⑦ Turn R at the first side road and follow it out of the village (600m). Turn L on the crossing path after the drive of Southwood Parks.

⑧ Follow the footpath under trees and between chalkpits to the field (100m) then on along the L edge (500m). Exit L at the end and carry on down the L edge past Southwood Farm R (400m). In the next field cross obliquely to the bottom corner and go out to the main road (500m).

⑨ Slightly R cross into the field. Diverge from the road to the edge of the trees and follow the path up over the shoulder of the hill to the edge of Alton (700m).

⑩ Go down the alleyway ahead between gardens (200m), over the road and on down Wentworth Gardens (100m). At the bottom, slightly L, walk down the grass to the next path (30m) then L to the 4-way path junction (20m).

⑪ Go R to the River Wey (200m) and out to the parking place.

10 Humbly Grove Oil Field and Weston Patrick

About 10 km/6 miles with an extension of 400m/¼ mile. The woodland part of the walk is best at bluebell time, April/May, before the brambles grow. OS maps 1:25000 44 Basingstoke, 1:50000 186 Aldershot.

Start from Weston Common where there is a small car park beside the oil field access road, SU 691 440. At Weston Patrick there are one or two roadside parking spots near the church, SU 690 470.

The Golden Pot ☎ 01420 80655

Linking walks 11☆ ㊸ ★

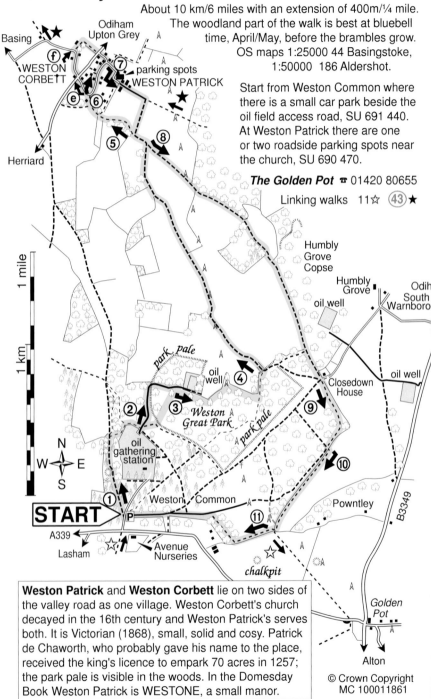

Weston Patrick and **Weston Corbett** lie on two sides of the valley road as one village. Weston Corbett's church decayed in the 16th century and Weston Patrick's serves both. It is Victorian (1868), small, solid and cosy. Patrick de Chaworth, who probably gave his name to the place, received the king's licence to empark 70 acres in 1257; the park pale is visible in the woods. In the Domesday Book Weston Patrick is WESTONE, a small manor.

© Crown Copyright MC 100011861

① Opposite the Weston Common car park, go down the bridleway diverging L from the Humbly Grove Oil Field road (500m). Just before the field L take the path R up to the fence of the oil gathering station (80m) and follow it round to the drive from the back gate (200m).

② Follow the drive L round a bend (300m) until the dip to the oil well (200m) (or go up the diverging path to the park pale (mound) of Weston Great Park (100m) and straight over the wood to the well (250m)).

③ Continue in the wood (without paths) R of the well enclosure and R of the zigzag edge of the next field to a pylon (400m) then outside two edges of a square of field to the track that has fields on both sides of it (400m).

④ Follow the track between fields, under power cables (450m) and round past a converging track R (1200m) to the R bend (100m).

⑤ Take the path ahead to the road bend in Weston Patrick (400m).

ⓔ *Extension of 400m/¼ mile: Go down L (150m), over the main road and up between the few houses of Weston Corbett to the footpath R just before the barns R (200m).*

ⓕ *Follow the path through the wood into the field (100m), round the corner R and down the edge to the road (150m). Keep on up the side road opposite (200m).* ➔⑦

⑥ Follow the road R to the T-junction (300m). Turn R (100m).

⑦ At the top, turn R to Weston Patrick Church (50m). Follow the the road round the churchyard to the barns (100m) and stay ahead up the farm track, round a R bend (200m), then a L bend (200m) to the track fork (100m).

⑧ Fork L down between fields. Keep to the same track up past the wood L (800m) and the next field L (350m) then in the R field beside Humbly Grove Copse (700m) and into the wood to the 5-way junction at Closedown House L (250m).

⑨ Continue up the path ahead curving R across a corner of wood to a forestry track on top (500m).

⑩ Turn L into the field and follow the R edge to the corner (650m). ☆

⑪ Re-enter the wood and follow the path outside the next field (200m) then R across the wood to the Forestry Commission hard track (200m). Walk along the track L to the car park (750m).

The **oil and gas** collected at the Humbly Grove oil field originated in the Lias shales of the Jurassic. These form the crumbling cliffs at Lyme Regis and were surmised to extend beneath the Hampshire chalk. The mud which turned into shale 200m years ago was rich in dead plankton dropped from the sea above. It had to sink 1½ miles into the earth's crust to achieve sufficiently high baking temperatures for the organic matter to form hydrocarbons. Oil and gas migrate through porous strata. In this oil field they have risen into reservoir rocks of the Great Oolite, a younger Jurassic layer which outcrops further north as Cotswold and Bath Stones. A geological trap is needed to prevent gas and oil dissipating. In Humbly Grove's case the trap is a horst - a block of crust faulted upwards between other blocks. This horst, part of the Weald deformity, was detected by seismic methods (measuring pulses reflected from surface explosions) during a deliberate hunt for oil traps in the 1970s.

Geology of the Humbly Grove Oilfield Hancock & Mithen, 15 in *Petroleum Geology of NW Europe*

11 Humbly Grove Oil Field and Shalden

About 8 km/5 miles with an extension of 3 km/2 miles; farmland and woods The woodland alternative with little change of length is for spring before the brambles grow. OS maps 1:25000 144 Basingstoke, 1:50000 186 Aldershot.

Start from Weston Common where there is a small car park beside the oil field access road, SU 691 440. In Shalden there is parking near the church.

Linking walks   8✧   9❈   10☆

The Golden Pot ☎ 01420 80655

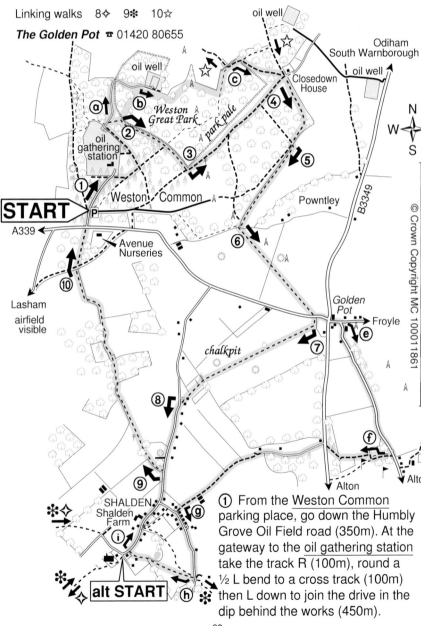

① From the Weston Common parking place, go down the Humbly Grove Oil Field road (350m). At the gateway to the oil gathering station take the track R (100m), round a ½ L bend to a cross track (100m) then L down to join the drive in the dip behind the works (450m).

ⓐ *Equal springtime alternative: Follow the drive L round a bend (300m) until the dip to the oil well (200m) (or go up the diverging path R to the park pale (linear mound) of Weston Great Park (100m) and over the wood to the well (250m)).*

ⓑ *Continue in the wood (without paths) R of the well and R of the zigzag edge of the next field to a pylon (400m) then outside two edges of a square past the track with fields on both sides (400m). ☆*

ⓒ *Follow the track R still inside the wood through the park pale (100m) then R across the wood to the 5-way junction at Closedown House (350m). Stay ahead. ➴④*

② Take the diverging path R up to the park pale (boundary mound) of Weston Great Park (100m) and follow it R to the end corner and a T-junction of paths (600m).

③ Go down the forest track L to the 5-way junction at Closedown House (900m). ☆ Turn R.

④ Ascend the path near the edge of the trees which curves R across a corner of the wood to a forestry track on top (500m).

⑤ Find the path L into the field and follow the R edge (650m).

⑥ In the next field turn back L and cross obliquely, diverging very slightly from the power lines to the mid-point of the hedge (350m). Go down the next field on the same line to join the road at the R edge, 100m before the corner (450m).

ⓔ *Extension of 3 km/2 miles: Go L (100m), over the crossroads and along the minor road beside the* **Golden Pot** *(60m). Turn R on the Alton side road. Follow it up the hill and down to the houses L (950m).*

ⓕ *In the wood R, just before the first house, Dormers, descend the track, or the path beside it (150m). At the golf course don't go on down the path but R up the track to the field (40m) then L along the edge and down through the trees to the main road (350m). Cross and carry on along the lane up past the houses. Stay ahead between fields and down to Shalden (1200m). ✳◈*

ⓖ *Walk L along the road to a footpath crossing after the drive of Southwood Park (600m). ✳*

ⓗ *Go R down the field, L of the pond, up between the gardens to the road near the church (450m). ◈*

ⓘ *Walk up through the village R past the side road (400m) and take the path L at the wood (200m). ➴⑨*

⑦ Cross into the field opposite. Follow the hedge outside the garden briefly (40m) then strike out R along the middle of the field parallel with the edge of the wood L and passing 50m L of the second chalkpit (clump of trees) (700m). Cross the end fence and follow the onward fences to the house drive (150m) near the road (30m).

⑧ Walk along the road L (300m) and take the path R at the end of the wood after the football field. ◈✳

⑨ Follow the path inside the edge of the wood (130m). Stay ahead across the end of the football field and through scrub (100m), along the L edge of the next field (400m), through the wood (200m) and on at the L edge of more fields (500m). After an S-bend continue on the other side of the hedge (200m).

⑩ Go straight up the wood to the road (300m) and along the oil field road to the car park R (100m).

12 Ropley and Kitwood

About 7½ km/4½ miles; undulating farmland and woods with long views. The extension of 2¼ km/1½ miles and short cut of 3 km/2 miles may be combined.

OS maps 1:25000 132 Winchester, 1:50000 ⎯ 186 Aldershot.

Start from Ropley recreation ground car park behind the Parish Hall, SU 642 320, or on the extension, from Swellinghill Pond, SU 662 329.

Linking walks
13 ♣ 14 ◇

Alresford
Winchester

Manor Farm

ridge

Old Down Wood

KITWOOD

alt START

Swellinghill Pond

vineyard

valley

parking spot

Lyew.
Far

START

parking spot

ridge

East Tist
A32

VH
ROPLEY

A31

valley

Petersfie

Merryfield Farm

West Tisted

© Crown Copyright
MC 100011861
·190m

① From the parish hall walk up through Ropley past the church (300m), the next side road L (150m) and one more house (40m).

② Take the path L of the pond to the fields (70m). Bear R down the fence (150m and cross the second field in the same oblique line to the protruding hedge corner (100m). Enter the next field.

ⓔ *Extension of 2¼ km/1½ miles to Swellinghill Pond:*
Keep to the same oblique line through the far L corner (200m), to the next protruding hedge corner near trees (250m) and down the small fields, R of a house (200m).

24

(f) *Cross the valley road and go up the R edge of the fields to the wood on the ridge (350m).*

(g) *In the top field follow the path R into the wood (30m) and stay ahead on the main winding path to a major cross path (500m).* ♣

(h) *Take the major path R to the end beside a house (400m). ✧ Go L on the road to the pond (150m).*

(i) *Take the path R of Swellinghill Pond (30m) and turn R. Don't go on round the pond but make for the hedge of the next field (50m). Go L beside the hedge (50m) and R into the field. Stay ahead to the corner between houses (150m).*

(j) *From the corner of the field follow the edge outside the garden and keep on at the R edge. When the RoW transfers to the side field R (250m), stay on the unofficial path in the field (500m). Carry on through trees (150m). At the track turn L to the road (60m).* ♦(4)

(3) Go straight over R of the hedge corner (150m) then diverge from the L hedge to the top edge 30m L of the R corner (300m). Cross the next field in the same line (150m) then bear R round beside the trees to the sunken track (150m). Turn R up the slope and stay ahead to the road (400m).

(4) Turn R along the road to the T-junction (200m). Cross the field opposite slightly R to the corner of the wood (500m) and carry on into the trees to the crosspath (30m).

(S) *Short cut of 3 km/2 miles: Turn R past the pond down the R edge of the wood (300m).*

(t) *Just before the road, turn R on the path to the field (50m). Keep on in the same oblique line across to*

the corner (200m), up the 2nd field to the middle of the end hedge (150m), across the 3rd field to 50m below the top corner (200m), then past the pylon (300m) to the corner between houses over the brow (400m). Turn R between hedges to the road (50m). Either go through the village (500m) or for ♦(2), cross to the path R of the house opposite.

(5) Stay ahead inside the L edge of the wood all the way down to the road (300m). Cross and drop to the lane below (40m). Walk down (R) to the end of the field (60m).

(6) Turn L to the large field (30m) and go up the L edge to the next road (350m). Cross slightly R to the farm drive and follow it to the barns (150m). Swing R to pass the L end of the houses (100m) and go on along the track (150m).

(7) Take the side track R into the wood (100m). Stay on this track past a side path up L between fields (550m) and watch out for a side path down R (100m) (150m before the trees at the road).

(8) Descend R to the next field (200m) and carry on, L of the house ahead, to the crossroads (300m). Continue on the tarmac road watching out for a path L (150m).

(9) Follow the path to the wood (100m) and turn R along the edge (250m). In the field go L past the end of the wood and straight over to the track in the trees (350m).

(10) Follow the track R down to the valley road below Ropley (500m).

(11) Turn L along the road (100m) and R up Church Lane (250m). Fork L up School Lane to the village street (200m) and turn L to the parish hall (100m).

13 Four Marks and Newton Common

About 7½ km/4¾ miles with a 3¼ km/2 mile extension via Kitwood; farmland and woods. OS maps 1:25000 132 Winchester, 1:50000 186 Aldershot.

Start in Four Marks from the kerbside in Weathermore Lane, SU 679 350, or walk out from the A31 on the footpath opposite the Medstead road.

Linking walk   12✿   14✦   15✿

The Windmill 01420 563554

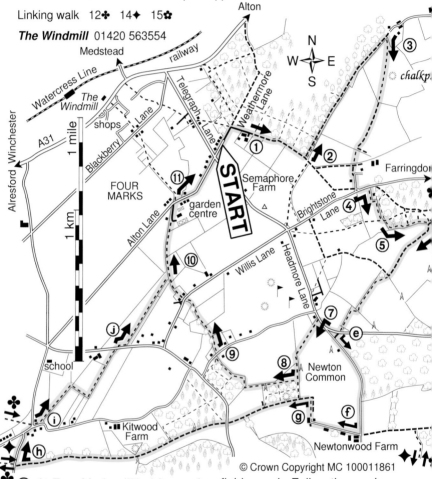

© Crown Copyright MC 100011861

① At Four Marks, (70m) beyond the tarmac in Weathermore Lane take the first side track R past the farm and keep on to the side track L at the end of the wood (550m).

② Follow the side track L along the edge of the wood all the way to the next houses (1000m).

③ Continue briefly on the lane for the view then return (100m) to the

field, now L. Follow the garden fence down and bear R into the dry valley near a chalkpit (tree clump). Walk up the valley to the hedge (550m). Go on up the drove track (300m). When it bends L towards the barns, stay ahead in the same line, over another track (100m), to the drive of Pies Farm (50m) and down to the road (120m).

26

④ Turn L down the road to the next house (100m) and R into the field before it. Follow the edge up round the garden and over the top, watching for access to the wood L just before the corner (250m).

⑤ In the wood, don't follow the right of way ahead but take the path R down round the edge of the wood to the bend in the large cart track (350m). ✿

⑥ Go up the track R, round the curve and on (500m). At the right angle bend enter the field ahead. Cross the R corner and follow the R edge (350m). Enter the next field L of the corner and converge on the R edge. Keep on to the road (200m).

ⓔ *Extension of 3¼ km/2 miles via Kitwood: go up the track opposite (50m). Turn L along the farm drive (private road/public footpath) to the 4-way junction (700m).* ✦

ⓕ *Turn R beside barns. Continue round the R bend, past the house (400m) and along the path to the track from the field (150m).*

ⓖ *Turn L. Stay ahead between fields and wood (600m), over the road, down the track opposite and up to the next road (1500m).* ♣

ⓗ *Walk along the road R to the T-junction at Kitwood (200m).*

ⓘ *Turn R to the next junction (50m) then take the footpath L of the road ahead. Follow it past the garden, along the R edge of the fields (400m), R across the end of the adjacent field (120m) and on as before down to the road (400m).*

ⓙ *Cross into the field opposite. Go round the R corner (50m) and up the R edge to the path outside the top edge (500m). Turn L.* ✦⑩

⑦ Walk along the road R (150m). At the garden L enter the corner of the field. Follow the hedge to the end and cross obliquely L to the far edge, 100m R of the pylon (300m), then take the footpath in the wood, past the pylon (100m).

⑧ After the pylon (70m) turn R through the wood (300m). Carry on at the edge of the field (100m) and R into the corner of the next wood. Follow the path down round the R edge to the road (300m).

⑨ Slightly R (20m) go up the L edge of the fields opposite and through the hedge on top (200m). Keep on at L edges down to the road (250m). Go straight on up between the houses and fields opposite (200m). A path joins L.

⑩ Stay on the path ahead to the garden centre (300m) and follow the track out to the road (150m).

⑪ Walk up the road (R) to Weathermore Lane (400m).

Moss is generally regarded as one plant but there are more than 900 species in Britain. Most are highly specific in habitat, living only on tree roots or rock or chalk soil in shade, etc.

The moss shown, *Mnium hornum*, carpets sandy soils under deciduous trees. Like most British mosses it sheds its spores in spring. The stalked capsule which produces the spores is a separate plant standing on top of its mother - the leafy part. A spore may blow far. It germinates to form a mass of threads which produce buds that grow into male or female leafy plants.

x2

14 Rotherfield Park and Kitwood

About 11½ km/7 miles. Farmland and woods on the Chalk, gently undulating.
OS maps 1:25000 132 Winchester, 1:50000 186 Aldershot.

Start at the layby in East Tisted, SU 702 332,
or at Swellinghill Pond, Kitwood, SU 662 329.

Linking walks   12◇   13◆   15★   16☆

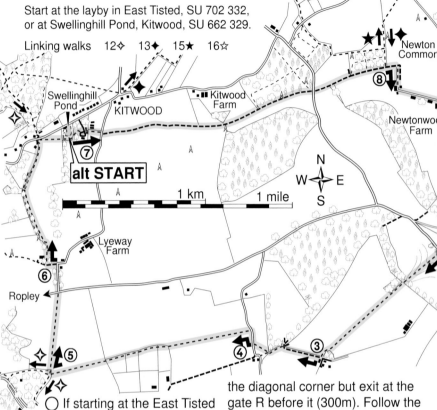

○ If starting at the East Tisted layby, walk down the village street past the church to the A32 (200m). Cross to the ornamental gates and go up the drive (50m) then L. ➔①

○ If starting at Swellinghill Pond, take the path away from the road R of the pond (30m). Don't go on round the pond but cross to the hedge of the R field (50m). Turn L near the hedge (50m) then L on the path out of the field. ➔⑦

① Turn across the Rotherwick Park grass above the lodge aiming for the hilltop L of the clump of trees (300m). In the next field turn R into the adjacent field (80m). Make for the diagonal corner but exit at the gate R before it (300m). Follow the track slightly L through the wood (250m) and carry on down the drive past a house to the road (150m). Turn R along the road watching out for a footpath up the cleft in the field L (350m).

② Follow the path up the dip to the corner of the wood R (350m). Carry on ahead past the end of the wood and straight over to the R edge of the next clump of trees (1000m). Keep on R of the trees to the end of the field (100m)

③ Outside the hedge, near a house, turn R on the track (250m). At the end of the R field, continue

28

ahead at the R edge of the next field to the end of the adjacent field (100m). Turn into the R field and cross obliquely to the road (100m).

© Crown Copyright MC 100011861

trees L but stay on the unofficial path inside the big field (400m). At hedge the RoW is in the adjacent field L but continue in the big field past the house to the corner (350m). Don't join the road but go round the corner R and diverge from the road to the stile at the trees, 100m from the road (150m).

⑦ Stay ahead on the path R of Swellinghill Pond winding through the trees and up into a garden (150m). Bear L between the sheds to the corner of the next field (50m) and go along the L edge to the road (100m). ✦ Slightly R (20m) go on along the track between fields to the next road (1500m). Cross and continue up the track R of the wood (600m).★

⑧ At the R bend after the wood, take the path R between hedges (120m). Join the estate road of Newtonwood Farm at the house and go round the L bend, past the barns (400m). At the drive junction stay ahead on the track between fields to the start of Plash Wood R (350m). ☆

⑨ Turn into the field R and follow the edge of the wood (250m). At the end of the field cross a corner of wood and carry on down the edge of the next field (250m). Stay beside the wood down the next field then up the slope L of the bridge (250m). Carry on outside the field in the trees to the drive from the house, Rotherfield Park (100m), and go down it to the lodge (500m).

④ Go R along the road. Watch out for a footpath L in the field (100m). Go straight across to the protruding hedge corner (600m), ahead L of the hedge through the small fields (500m) and over to the wood 30m L of the R corner (400m). ✧✧

⑤ At the wood turn R across the same field, aiming slightly R for the gateway at the end of a row of trees (500m). Outside, take the lane opposite to the bend (200m).

⑥ Turn L on the track and R on the path in the trees after the R field (60m). Follow the path through the trees (150m) and carry on along the L edge of the field. After the pylon the right-of-way is behind the

• If returning to Swellinghill Pond turn R just before the lodge. ✦①
• If returning to East Tisted carry on to the A32 (50m) and go up the village street to the layby (200m).

15 Farringdon and Newton Common

About 9¾ km/6 miles over arable farmland with an extension of ¾ km/½ mile to Newton Valence. OS maps 1:25000 132 + 133, 1:50000 186 Aldershot.

Start from Lower Farringdon car park, SU 706 350, or park at the roadside near the *Rose & Crown* in Upper Farringdon, SU 715 350. On the extension park near the ponds in Newton Valence, SU 723 327.

Linking walks 13✿ 14★ 16❋ 17❋ 19❋ 20◇

The Pheasant ☎ 01420 588255
The Rose & Crown ☎ 01420 588231

© Crown Copyright MC 100011861

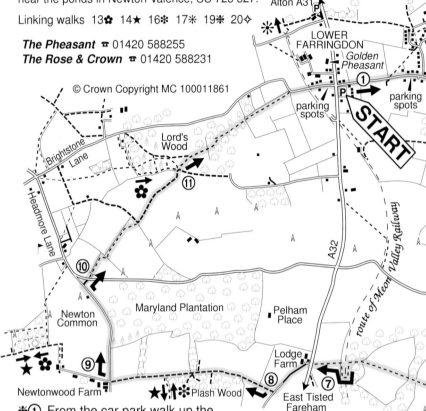

❋① From the car park walk up the road to Upper <u>Farringdon</u> (600m). After the side road L watch for the bridleway R from a drive (200m).

② Go up the bridleway to the R bend then ahead up the bank and obliquely L up the fields aiming for the L corner of the hedge near the top of the hill (350m). R of the corner cross the track and go on in the same line over the top field and down to the L corner (300m).

③ Drop to the next field and follow the winding hedge L (400m). ◇

④ Just before the wood turn R down on the track from the top field, into the (dry) valley and up to the farm and road (850m).

ⓔ *Extension of ¾ km/½ mile to Newton Valence: Go up the road R (100m). Take the path L next to the octagonal house. Keep to the slight valley up the field (400m). Over the drive continue ½R up the next field, R of the line of trees (100m). Carry on R of the garden hedge to the drive near the church (50m).* ❋

(f) *Turn R to the road (70m) and R along it to the last house (300m).*

(g) *Climb into the field L and cross ½R to the gateway near the pines (in line with the distant large house, Rotherfield Park)(200m). Keep on to the bend in the drive after the house (200m) and into the field ahead.* ➔(6)

Rose & Crown

UPPER FARRINGDON

(2)

N
W ✦ E
S

(3) (4)

Newton House

(5) (e)
Newton Valence
Place Farm

NEWTON
VALENCE

Shotters
Farm (g) (f)

(6)

alt START

(5) Go R up the lane (300m), over the crossroads and up to Shotters Farm (250m). When the lane bends L round the house, turn R.

(6) Cross the field along the top of the slope, past the pylon into the wood (600m). Keep straight on through the belt of trees and over another field to a bight in the edge (400m), into the wood and down to

the disused cutting of the Meon Valley Railway (150m).

(7) The right-of-way continues opposite but it may be easier to follow the cutting down L and return up the other side (200m). Go on across the field (200m) and over the road into the drive of Lodge Farm (40m). Take the track ½L up the valley side onto tarmac (300m).

> The large house above, Pelham Place, was built in 1782 for Admiral Thomas Dumaresq, a Jersey man, 1728-1802. He had been captain of the Repulse under Rodney at the Battle of the Saints. An admiral received $1/8$ of the prize money won by all the ships under his command.

(8) Halfway up, turn R on the track between fields. Go over the top, to the end of Plash Wood L (800m) ★ and on to the junction of drives at Newtonwood Farm (400m). ✿

(9) Follow the drive R (700m).

(10) After the house (80m) turn R on the track (50m) and cross the road into the field opposite. Follow the L edge then cut the corner to the exit 50m R (200m). Likewise in the next field - along the L edge then R over the corner to the exit (350m). Join the track under the trees and continue ahead, eventually down L to the complex junction in the little valley (500m).

(11) Don't go round the bend but up the R path into the wood on the other side of the valley. Various forestry tracks cross. Always take track or path most nearly ahead to the end of the wood (600m). Continue down the L edge of the field to the road (400m) ✳ and ahead to the main road in Lower Farringdon (300m). Cross to the car park (50m).

16 Newton Valence and East Tisted

About 8¾ km/5½ miles; hilly farm and parkland; long views; muddy in winter.
OS maps 1:25000 132 Winchester +133 Basingstoke, 1:50000 186 Aldershot.

Start at Newton Valence; park on the verge near the ponds, SU 723 327.
Alternatively start from the layby in East Tisted, SU 702 322.

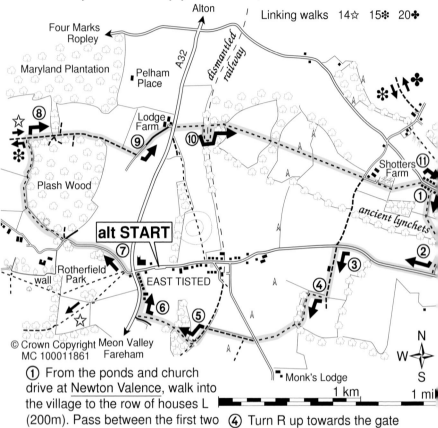

© Crown Copyright MC 100011861

① From the ponds and church drive at <u>Newton Valence</u>, walk into the village to the row of houses L (200m). Pass between the first two into the field and carry on down the L edge (200m), and down the first <u>lynchet</u>. In the next field descend obliquely L to the trees R of the end hedge in the field below (200m). Drop through the trees on the next lynchet then go L round the corner of the field and along the end hedge to the road (200m).

② Walk along the road R (700m).

③ Take the first L track up past the barn (150m) and into the next field (200m).

④ Turn R up towards the gate (100m) then L beside the trees (250m). At the corner cross the band of trees to the field R above. Aim straight up over the hilltop to the gate in the hedge, 150m L of the top pylon (300m). Cross the road and go on along the track at the top edge of the field, past a descending side path L (50m). Keep on to the end and out (200m).

⑤ Follow the track L (120m) then bear R on the path around outside the end of the R field. Stay ahead through the trees to the next field (250m), along the tree-lined L edge, above the valley, and directly down to the gate at the road (250m).

⑥ Walk along the verge R (100m), then the pavement, to the side road in East Tisted (200m).

⑦ Cross the main road and enter the gates of Rotherfield Park. Walk up the winding drive (500m). When it bends L to the bridge and house, avoid the tracks R and stay ahead on the path through the edge of the wood to the field (100m). Keep to the R edge of the fields beside Plash Wood up to the track along the top edge of the wood (750m). ✽

⑧ Turn R along the track (800m). The large house far L is Pelham Place.

⑨ At the end turn L down to the farm (300m). Cross the main road (40m) and go straight up the field (200m) into the wood.

⑩ The path continues on the far side of the disused cutting of the Meon Valley Railway but you may find it more convenient to descend R and return up the other side (200m). Carry on up through the wood (150m). Continue across the field slightly R to the gap at the middle of the far edge and pass through the belt of trees to the next field (400m). Go straight over past the (highest) pylon and on through the next field to the gate 40m R of the L corner (600m). ✤ Still ahead, follow the drive behind Shotters Farm which becomes a track to a field (200m). Cross ½L to the corner near the houses of Newton Valence (250m).

⑪ Drop to the road and walk through the village R to the ponds and the church drive (300m).

START

NEWTON VALENCE

Selborne

Selborne

East Tisted became a manor when Richard I granted land from Tisted and Selborne to Adam de Gurdon I in the 1190s. The TISTEDE in the Domesday Book is West Tisted. A writ of 1218 survives for the sheriff to seize the estate from Adam de Gurdon II. The Hundred Roll of 1275 lists OSTEDE as held for half a knight's fee and having the freedom to hunt wolves and hares. The Nortons acquired the manor by bequest in 1309 and united it with Rotherfield by marriage in 1495. The village stretches between the church and the (ex-) Meon Valley Railway. The church, St James, was largely rebuilt in 1846 but the chancel arch and base of the tower are early 14th century work. Points of interest: 16th & 17th century tombs of the Nortons, Queen Anne's arms 1706, the cast iron fleur de lys finials on the pews, endowment notices in the tower.

Rotherfield Park is a Victorian Gothic house, the towers being added in the 1880s to the main building of 1820; parts of earlier houses remain. The estate first comes to light in a pipe roll of 1166 as a manor of Richard de Rotherfield. A descendant married Richard Norton in 1495 uniting the manor with East Tisted. The Scott family has owned Rotherfield Park since 1808.

Adam de Gurdon (d.1305) was a notable medieval figure who lived locally. He was on the losing side with Simon de Montfort (Castellan of Odiham) in the Barons' War with Henry III. Outlawed in 1266, he became part of a band of raiders. Single combat against Edward I at Alton Wood (or Halton Bucks), wisely lost, brought him back to royal favour. He got his lands back, fought in the Welsh and Scottish wars, was appointed Justice of the Forest in 1280 and became Custos of the Hampshire Shore in 1295. His first wife was Constantia de Venuz of Worldham. His father (Adam II) was the King's Bailiff of Alton.

17 Chawton and Farringdon

About 8¼ km/5 miles with an extension of 1½ km/1 mile. Jane Austen's home; farm country. OS maps 1:25000 133 Haslemere, 1:50000 186 Aldershot.

Start from the village car park in Chawton, SU 708 375, or the long cul-de-sac. On the extension there is a car park and an A32 layby at Lower Farringdon.

Linking walks   7✿   15✳   18❖   19✴

The Greyfriar ☎ 01420 83841   **The Golden Pheasant** ☎ 01420 588255
The Rose & Crown ☎ 01420 588231   Jane Austen's House ☎ 01420 83262

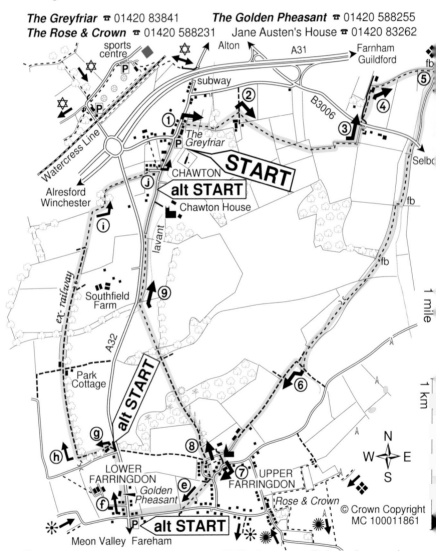

① From Chawton car park turn R past the **Greyfriar** along the road (100m). Take the path R between gardens, straight across fields

(200m), over a ditch and up under trees (50m). In the top field aim ½L past the farm and cross the track into the next field (200m).

34

② Cut the corner R to the next field and continue on the same oblique line from stile to stile over several fields to exit at a gate (600m) then follow the L edge to the track near houses (350m).

③ Turn L to the road and cross into the field opposite (150m). Stay ahead on the R track (250m).

④ After the shed turn R over the field beside the hedge. Cross the brook to the drive (450m). ❖

⑤ Follow the drive R to the road (nasty crossing) (500m). Slightly R (20m) cross into the field opposite. Stay ahead L of the stream to the footbridge (400m) then on the R side to the bridge at end of the wood (400m) then on the L side to the end of the fields (800m). Keep on to the major farm track (150m).

⑥ Go R on the track, round the L bend (50m) and over the shoulder of the hill, past the barns, to Manor Farm house R (800m). ✳✳

⑦ Walk down L past Farringdon Church (100m), R on the road and just into Parsonage Close (150m).

ⓔ *Extension of 1½ km/1 mile via Lower Farringdon: Take the track L to the fields. At the bend, turn L on the oblique footpath across the fields (300m) then walk down the road to Lower Farringdon (400m).*

ⓕ *Cross the A32 and follow it R past the* **Golden Pheasant** *(150m) to the edge of the village (300m).*

ⓖ *In the first field L skirt round the buildings then follow the L edge to the track in the trees (300m) - the route of the Meon Valley railway.*

ⓗ *Turn R on the track then stay ahead: past a cross track near Park Cottage (600m), under a farm track bridge (600m) into a field,*

where the track bends L (250m) and on to the bottom end of the next hedge (250m).

ⓘ *Turn R down to the R end of the trees (100m) then L along the spinney (100m) into the next field. Go down the R edge and over the road (200m). Stay ahead R of the field, between gardens and along the Close to the T-junction (250m).*

ⓙ *Turn L into Chawton (200m).*

⑧ Take the path R, past houses to the cross track (150m). Stay ahead up between fields, through the wood on top (500m), down between fields, through a belt of trees into the corner of the next field (300m) and obliquely down to the bottom corner, over the lavant near the bottom (250m).

⑨ Go on outside the fields to the village street (450m) and ahead past Chawton Church (250m) to Jane Austen's House (450m).

Jane Austen, 1775-1817, was born at Steventon where her father was rector. He took pupils which may account for her good education. Her mother and sister were both named Cassandra. Two brothers became parsons and two became admirals. Another took the name Knight on inheriting estates in Kent, Steventon and Chawton. After their father retired, the sisters lived in Bath with their parents. When he died the ladies moved to Southampton but in 1809 settled at Chawton. Jane's last weeks were spent in lodgings at Winchester to be near her physician; she was buried in the Cathedral. Four novels were published anonymously and the other two were posthumous. Before she died she had earned £700 but only anonymous fame. *Pride and Prejudice, Northanger Abbey & Sense and Sensibility* were published from Chawton but written at Steventon.

18 Upper Farringdon and West Worldham

About 10 km/6¼ miles with an extension of 1½ km/1mile over Windmill Hill and an extension of ½ km/¼ mile to Hartley Mauditt; rolling farmland on the Chalk. OS maps 1:25000 133 Haslemere, 1:50000 186 Aldershot.

Start at a roadside parking spot near the *Rose & Crown* in Upper Farringdon, SU 715 350 or, on the extension, near Hartley Mauditt church, SU 742 361.

Linking walks   17❖   19★   21✪   27◇   38★

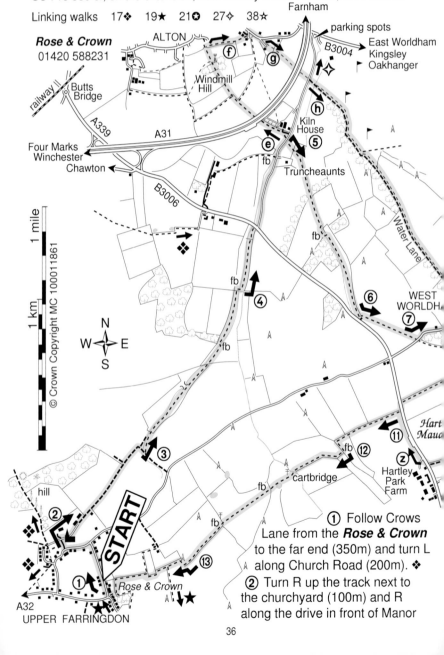

Rose & Crown
01420 588231

① Follow Crows Lane from the **Rose & Crown** to the far end (350m) and turn L along Church Road (200m). ❖

② Turn R up the track next to the churchyard (100m) and R along the drive in front of Manor

36

Farm house (200m). After the barns stay ahead on the farm track down to the R bend (600m).

③ Just round the bend (50m) take the footpath L (150m) and carry on along the fields, R of the stream. At the wood L (750m) cross the footbridge and continue L of the stream (400m).

④ At the end of the field cross the footbridge and continue R of the stream (450m) to a nasty road crossing. Slightly R (20m), carry on along the tarmac drive past the house Truncheaunts (500m), over the stream and ahead towards Kiln House (200m). ✧

ⓔ *Extension of 1½ km/1 mile over Windmill Hill: At Kiln House take the path L (250m). Cross the A31 and go straight up over the hilltop, through trees to houses (650m).*

ⓕ *Turn R along the path beside the gardens to the road (300m).*

ⓖ *Go R down the hill and into the 1st drive R (100m). Before the house branch L down the path over the A31 to the drive (400m).*

ⓗ *Go straight on over the bridge and up the edge of the golf course into the top R corner (800m). Stay at the edge of the fields up to the road (1200m). Turn L ➜⑧*

lt START

⑤ About 50m before Kiln House, cross the stream R and walk up the fields to the hedge and ditch (150m). Follow the ditch up R to the wood (550m) then cross into the field L but carry on in the same direction up the narrowing field. Converge on the L hedge and follow it round to the road (600m).

⑥ Don't join the road but diverge L from it over the large field up to the next road. Aim for the R edge of the wood at the top (500m).

⑦ Walk along the road L to West Worldham (500m).

⑧ Opposite the church, turn R on the side road. ★ Go on round the bend to the next side road (300m).

ⓧ *Extension of ½ km/¼ mile: Stay on the road ahead (600m).* ✪

ⓨ *Just before Hartley Mauditt Church take the R track (600m).*

ⓩ *Turn R along the road or the grass border of the L field. At the end of the field (450m) turn L. ➜⑪*

⑨ Turn R down the edge of the field beside the garden (250m).

⑩ At the end of the fence, turn L (10m) and climb into the adjacent field L. Follow the hedge R (200m) round the R bend and down to the road (500m). Cross and join the path on the other side (50m L).

⑪ Walk down beside the R hedge (400m) and ahead into the corner of the next field (100m).

⑫ Go L round the corner (70m) and cross the footbridge R. Carry on along the bank of the deep stream at the L edge and over the cart bridge (400m). Look ahead for the 2nd line of pylons and a hilltop ½R. Identify the pylon 2nd L from the hilltop and aim for it, R of the pond (200m) and across the next field (450m). The exit is at a Z-bend in the high hedge, 70m L of the end of the high part. Keep on ahead to the end of the L hedge (400m). ★

⑬ After the pylon follow the R edge along the field almost to the village (550m). At the end of the field go round the corner L (80m) and out R to Crows Lane (80m).

19 Selborne and Upper Farringdon

About 9½ km/5¾ miles through farmland and woods. Selborne Common may cause confusion. OS maps 1:25000 133 Haslemere, 1:50000 186 Aldershot

Start from the public car park behind the *Selborne Arms*, SU 741 335, or from the roadside in Farringdon near the *Rose & Crown*, SU 715 350.

Linking 15✳ 17✻ 18★ 20✿ 21✳ 22✿ 24★

The Selborne Arms ☎ 01420 511247
The Queens Hotel ☎ 01420 511454
The Rose & Crown ☎ 01420 588231
Gilbert White Museum ☎ 01420 511275

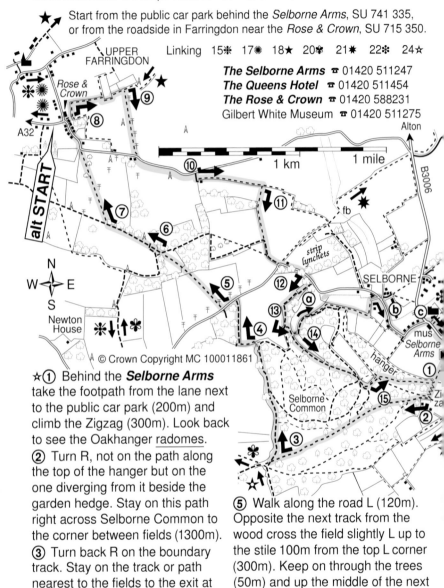

© Crown Copyright MC 100011861

★① Behind the **Selborne Arms** take the footpath from the lane next to the public car park (200m) and climb the Zigzag (300m). Look back to see the Oakhanger radomes.

② Turn R, not on the path along the top of the hanger but on the one diverging from it beside the garden hedge. Stay on this path right across Selborne Common to the corner between fields (1300m).

③ Turn back R on the boundary track. Stay on the track or path nearest to the fields to the exit at the corner of the wood (850m). ✿

④ Go L along the top edge of the field into the wood (100m) then R down the track inside the edge of the wood to the road (300m).

⑤ Walk along the road L (120m). Opposite the next track from the wood cross the field slightly L up to the stile 100m from the top L corner (300m). Keep on through the trees (50m) and up the middle of the next field to the top L corner (100m). ✳

⑥ Outside, follow the horse track L, soon between fields (150m). After the pylon R continue to the side path in the next field R (300m).

38

⑦ Go down through the middle of the field to the bottom L corner (500m) and L along the road in Upper Farringdon (200m). ※★

⑧ Beside the **Rose & Crown** take the footpath into the field (60m) then follow the L edge round the corner (80m) and on towards a pylon (450m).

⑨ Before the pylon turn R over the field towards a house (400m). Turn L along the road. Pass under power cables and round a L curve to the next house (400m).

⑩ Turn R into the drive (30m) and L outside the garden. Keep on at the R hedge (400m). Watch out for the stile R opposite the corner of the wood over the next field. ※

⑪ Cross towards the corner of the wood (100m) and go up the R edge of the field near it, over the ridge, and down to the road (600m). Descend L (300m).

⑫ Take the first track R up to the field (150m). Follow the L edge (100m) then descend through the trees to the path junction (120m).

⑬ Drop L, down, round to the narrow fields (70m).

ⓐ *Alternative route (same length) through* Selborne *village: Pass between the fields (30m) then turn L. Follow the winding path beside fields all the way to the road. It passes out of the wood (400m), down between fields (200m), round a L bend (100m) and R on the drive to Fisher Lodge (100m).*

ⓑ *Walk along the road R and round the L bend to the main street (350m) near the* Gilbert White Museum, *Plestor and church.*

ⓒ *Follow the village street R to the Selborne Arms (300m).*

⑭ Don't pass between the fields but outside (R of) the narrow one. Avoid R turns and go up through the wood to join a converging path near a bank (lynchet) L (500m).

⑮ Go up the path in sight of the lynchet. Don't take any R turns but follow the main path round the end of the lynchet L (100m) to the brow of Selborne Hanger (100m). Cross the brow path and bear R down the slanting path to the path junction at the bottom of the Zigzag (400m). Turn L to the *Selborne Arms* (200m). ✿

Rushes are plants of waterlogged soils. They are not grasses. Most species grow as dense tufts. The inflorescence appears to be some way down the stem but it is a leaf which projects above it.

The cells of the pith are stellate with so much space between them that the stem is mainly air. Water plants always have large air spaces, presumably to allow the roots to snorkel.

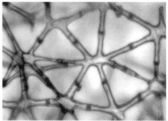

The air spaces allow a dried rush to absorb molten fat like a wick - the basis for rush lights. Gilbert White in *The Natural History* describes the preparation of the rush, *Juncus conglomeratus*. He experimented to find the cost of the light - a farthing for 5½ hours using bought rushes and bought fat. A long rush would burn for more than an hour. The very poor, "always the worst œconomists", had only two hours of light from their halfpenny candles.

20 Selborne and Newton Valence

About 7½ km/4¾ miles with an extension of 1 km/¾ mile; rolling arable land and woods with long views. OS 1:25000 133 Haslemere, 1:50000 186 Aldershot

Start from the public car park behind the *Selborne Arms*, SU 741 335.

The Selborne Arms ☎ 01420 511247
The Queens Hotel ☎ 01420 511454
Gilbert White Museum ☎ 01420 511275

Linking walks   15◇   16♣
19❀   21◆   22☆   24❖

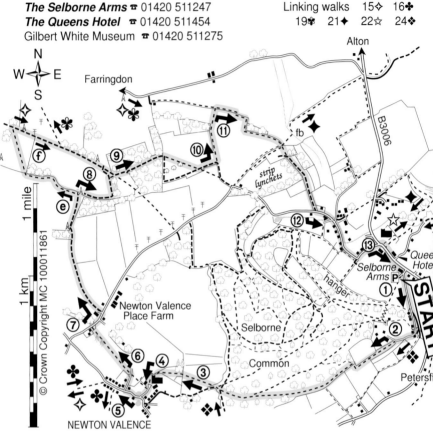

❖① At the *Selborne Arms* follow the side lane away from the street past houses R (350m), round the 1st R bend and up steeply (150m).
② At the next bend, 100m below the next house, take the footpath L along the narrow field to Selborne Common. In the next field follow the top edge (300m) and round R into the trees. Stay on the path along the hillside (800m). Join the path converging R and keep on to the end of the Common (200m).

③ Cross the boundary path to the gateway. Outside take the path R of the track into the field. Go straight over, L of the clump of trees to the narrow end of the next field (450m).
④ Don't continue into the field ahead but take the path L through the trees to Newton Valence church (50m). Follow the manor house drive to the road (100m). ◇♣
⑤ Walk along the road R (150m) and turn down the tarmac drive R after the first house R (150m).

⑥ At the start of the fields a path crosses the drive. Go down the L field in the slight valley and out R of the octagonal cottage (400m). Walk down the road R (100m).

⑦ Turn L down the track between the barns and house. Stay on the main track into the bottom of the dry valley and up L of the hillside wood to the field on top (850m).

ⓔ *Extension of 1 km/¾ mile: Take the path L outside the hedge down then up. Watch out for a gap into the field above R after the clump of trees (400m). Cross the field to the track along the far edge. The right-of-way is oblique to 80m L of the pylon (300m).* ❧

ⓕ *Turn back R along the track between fields into the wood and round a L bend (800m).* ➤⑨

⑧ Follow the track R at the edge of the field (250m). Go L round the 1st corner but just before the top corner exit R into the wood (120m).

⑨ Keep on along track (or small side paths if muddy) to the end of the wood (400m). At the field, aim slightly R to pass L of the isolated tree and down to the bottom track near a bend in the hedge (300m).

⑩ Continue along the cart track L to the end of the field (120m) then turn L. Follow the edge of the R field down R of trees (250m) and cross towards the stile (100m).

⑪ Turn R along the hedge. The RoW is on the other side of the hedge but crosses back to this side (150m). Carry on round R & L bends to the end of the field, out through the corner of the hedge at the 4-way path junction (600m) ✦ and straight up the next field (80m). Carry on over the top, through the narrow field and down the track to the road (120m).

⑫ Follow the road L past Fisher Lodge (100m) ✦ and on round the bend (350m) to the main street (200m), near the Gilbert White Museum, Plestor and church. ☆

⑬ Walk through the village, R, to the *Selborne Arms* (300m).

Gilbert White,1720-93, is known for his book, *The Natural History and Antiquities of Selborne in the County of Southampton*, published in 1789 and in print ever since. It has been translated into every major language.

In the book he recorded observations and research. He travelled frequently and widely in England writing detailed journals and copious letters which have been published. They provide a picture of country life and lore used as a source for social history as well as natural history. His writing was novel in that he noticed phenomena that needed explaining and was objective in his speculation and research. The memorial window in Selborne Church contrives a parallel with Francis of Assisi but Gilbert White's attitudes were scientific, not sentimental or saintly. If he wanted to know what a bird ate, he shot one to look inside it.

He had six brothers and four sisters; his father was a barrister and his grandfather was Vicar of Selborne. In infancy his home was at Compton under the Hogs Back. While at school he lived with his brother at Marelands in Bentley. He became a fellow of Oriel College and a curate of nearby Farringdon (the living of Selborne was in the gift of Magdalen). When appointed Vicar of Moreton-Pinkney in Northamptonshire, he employed a curate to carry out his church duties so that he could live in Selborne.

The Natural History of Selborne Gilbert White Thames and Hudson 1993 256pp

21 Selborne, Hartley Mauditt and Wick Hill

About 8½ km/5¼ miles with an extension of 1 km/¾ mile and a short cut of 1½ km/1 mile; undulating farmland and woods with good views; nettles in summer. OS maps 1:25000 133 Haslemere, 1:50000 186 Aldershot.

Start from the public car park behind the *Selborne Arms*, SU 741 335, or from a parking spot near Hartley Mauditt Church, SU 742 361.

The Selborne Arms ☎ 01420 511247
The Queens Hotel ☎ 01420 511454
Gilbert White Museum 01420 511275

Linking walks 18✪ 19✳ 20✦
22✳ 23✳ 24✪ 27✿ 38✪

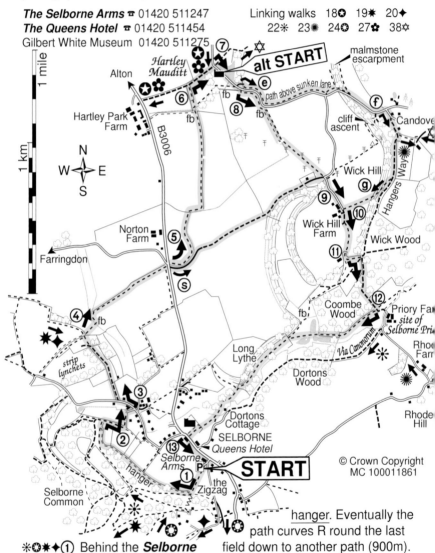

© Crown Copyright
MC 100011861

✳✪✳✦① Behind the *Selborne Arms*, take the path between the lane and the car park (200m). At the foot of the Zigzag turn R along the path beside fields below the hanger. Eventually the path curves R round the last field down to another path (900m). ② Turn R and R again (150m). Pass round a L bend (100m) and turn R along the drive to reach the road at Fishers Lodge (350m).

42

③ Follow the road L (120m). Just before the next house L bear R up the sunken track (130m). Carry on up the long field (strip lynchets), over the ridge and ahead down the next field to the hedge (500m).

④ Over the fence turn R across the corner of the field down to the cart bridge (100m). Cross it and go L beside the ditch, round bends (80m) and up beside the hedge and deep malmstone ravine to the road junction (600m).

Ⓢ *Short cut of 1½ km/1 mile: Go up the farm track opposite. After the concrete (250m) keep on to the end of the field (500m) then along the top of the hanger (350m) and past houses out to the road bend (130m). Turn R.* ➔Ⓨ

⑤ Opposite, don't follow the track but climb into the corner of the field slightly L. Follow the deep ravine up round the field to the top corner (500m) and carry on round the R edge in the next field (700m). In the dip at the top corner cross the footbridge to the next field. Carry on ahead on top of the bank to the cart track (150m). ✪

⑥ Go R to the little road (200m).✿

⑦ Turn R along the road past Hartley Mauditt Church to the end of the pond (150m). ✱

ⓔ *Extension of 1 km/¾ mile: After the pond (50m) take the track L through trees into the field (50m). Follow the edge round above the road, past the exit at the side road R (650m), to the hanger (80m) then down beside the trees to the road (70m) and ahead (300m).*

ⓕ *Turn R on the tarmac drive at Candovers (the Hangers Way) (70m), then bear R on the track*

skirting the houses. Disregard the entrances to the field and keep on below the hanger (400m).

ⓖ *Halfway along the fields, at the dividing fence, fork R up the malm-scarp (200m) and cross the field to Wick Hill Farm (200m). Turn L* ➔⑩

⑧ After the pond (100m) when the lane curves L, enter the large field R. Follow the L edge round the R corner (100m) and L bend (100m). then cross to the adjacent field L Keep on L of the hedge & ditch to the culverted crossing of the ditch (200m) then diverge from the hedge. Aim via the electricity pole for the top of the field L of the house and garden (400m).

⑨ Join the lane at the bend and go up past Wick Hill Farm (250m).

⑩ Continue on the track from the end of the tarmac past the field R, down between hedges to the end (300m) and down the neck of the next field (50m).

⑪ Go L along the edge of the field to the track in the trees (150m) and R down the track (400m).

⑫ Enter the next field R, above Priory Farm. Follow the top edge next to the wood (300m) then go through the edge of the wood to the next corner (150m). Pass between the ponds and keep on over the field up to the edge of the wood then ahead beside it (250m). Go on through the valleyside wood (Long Lythe). Don't turn R at the next field (500m). After Dortons Cottage L cross the stream ahead and go up the L path to Selborne Church (250m) then out through the Plestor to the road (150m).

⑬ Walk through the village L to the car park (300m).

22 Selborne Zigzag and Priory Farm

About 6½ km/4 miles; steep slopes; woodland and farmland. Good for wild flowers in spring. OS maps 1:25000 133 Haslemere, 1:50000 186 Aldershot.

Start from the public car park behind the *Selborne Arms*, SU 741 335.

Linking walks 19❋ 20☆ 21❋ 23✿ 24❀

The Selborne Arms ☎ 01420 511247
The Queens Hotel ☎ 01420 511454
Gilbert White Museum ☎ 01420 511275

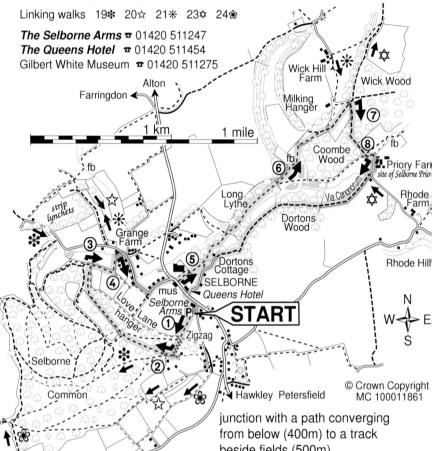

© Crown Copyright
MC 100011861

❋☆❀① Behind the **Selborne Arms**, take the path from the lane next to the car park (200m). Climb the Zigzag to the top (300m).

② From the stone on top follow the path R beside the garden hedge (80m). Just after the hedge corner bear R, slightly downwards, into the trees on the edge of the chalk escarpment. The path follows the top of Selborne Hanger, rising briefly, then sloping down past the

junction with a path converging from below (400m) to a track beside fields (500m).

③ Follow the track down R beside the fields (200m), round a L bend (100m) and turn R on the drive past Fisher Lodge (100m). ❋

④ Walk along the lane R (350m) and round a L bend up to the main street of the village (200m) near the Gilbert White Museum.

⑤ Cross the main road and go up through the Plestor to Selborne Church (100m). Carry on out of the far corner of the churchyard and

44

down the field, over the Seale Stream and L of Dortons Cottage (200m). Keep on beside the hillside wood, the Long Lythe (600m).

⑥ At the next field the path forks. Take the upper path L to the corner of the wood (150m) then down R to the footbridge (60m) and up L to the top corner of the wood on the other side of the little valley (120m). Continue on the track along the top edge of the wood to the next field (250m) and cross to the far corner (200m). ✿

⑦ Join the track outside and follow it back down R through the wood to Priory Farm (500m).

⑧ Cross the stream and follow the concrete track skirting the buildings (150m). After the farmhouse drive don't take the lane L but continue ahead on the track (Via Canonorum) up through the valley to Dortons Cottage (1300m) then the tarmac lane up the malmscarp into Selborne (300m). The *Selborne Arms* is L. through the village (100m).

The Zigzag path up through Selborne Hanger was laid out by Gilbert White and his brother. It climbs a chalk escarpment - geologically the very end of the Weald, the long narrow dome of strata whose other end is under Canterbury.

Looking across Selborne from the top of the Zigzag, the next hill, with Wick Hill Farm on it, is part of the malmstone shelf which protrudes from under the chalk. The fringe of trees is the top of the hanger on the precipitous edge of the shelf - the malmstone escarpment. The village stands on the shelf where it is narrow because streams have cut a valley across it - down to the Gault Clay at Priory Farm. The radomes of Oakhanger obtrude at the foot of the Gault clay pastures and the edge of the Greensand heath of Woolmer Forest.

Malmstone is the white stone of the church and old houses in Selborne. It is a highly calcareous sandstone of the Upper Greensand analogous with Reigate Stone and clunch. It looks like chalk but flakes with weathering and feels like fine sand paper when rubbed whereas chalk is hardly ever used in exterior walls and feels smooth. The Exchequer accounts for 1369 (Edward III) itemize 825 feet of stone brought from Bentley for work on Odiham Castle.

The malmstone escarpment, "malmscarp", is often almost vertical because of quarrying and cliff falls. The Gault beneath it allows the edge to be undermined by weathering and causes slippage. Gilbert White describes a portion breaking loose near Hawkley in 1774 after a wet winter. It slipped 181 yards disturbing 50 acres of ground and leaving a precipice 23 yards high. He also records that the *lythes* were steep slopes used for sheep grazing.

The malmstone shelf extends round to Binsted and Bentley where it has been cleft by the valley of the River Wey. Around the Worldhams it is more than a mile wide, riddled with little ravines. The last hops grew on it and it provides a very fertile soil with much evidence of prehistoric agriculture.

23 Oakhanger, Rhode and Candovers

About 8½ km/5¼ miles with an extension of ¾ km/½ mile. Round the satellite control stations on farmland, woods and confusing heath. Shady in summer; boggy in winter. OS maps 1:25000 133 Haslemere, 1:50000 186 Aldershot.

Start in Oakhanger from the village green, SU 770 362, or from the *Red Lion*.

Linking walks   21✹   22✿   38★

The Red Lion ☎ 01420 472232

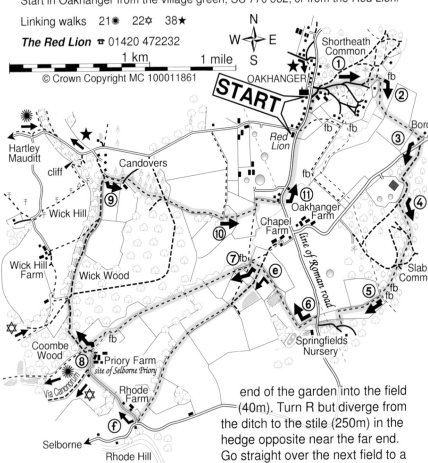

① From the corner of the village green, away from the road, a major track curves R to houses. Near the start of it (30m) take the 2nd side track L into Shortheath Common. Disregard a branch track R (150m) and carry on (100m). Just before the cottage, Waterside, fork L. Soon after the bend (60m), fork R.

② When the path bends L (60m), fork R over the footbridge at the end of the garden into the field (40m). Turn R but diverge from the ditch to the stile (250m) in the hedge opposite near the far end. Go straight over the next field to a projecting corner and on beside the hedge (300m) then between gardens to the road (50m).

③ Walk along the verge R (50m) then cross and follow the army track diverging from the road into Slab Common (250m). Just before the satellite control station, follow the L bend and continue around the perimeter fence (200m) watching out for a path L through the trees.

46

④ Follow this path through the common to fields. It crosses a track (250m). At the next track (150m) it re-starts slightly R (20m) near the track junction. Stay ahead to the footpath that skirts the fields at the edge of the common (250m).

⑤ Slightly L enter the field and follow the R hedge to the end of the adjacent field R (200m). A bit further on, in line with the radome (80m), cross the bridge and field L to the stile (50m) and go out through the trees (30m). Turn R to the drive from the house (50m) and follow it (R) to the road (150m).

⑥ Cut R through the Springfield Nursery car park or go R along the road (70m). Turn L along the end of the car park and keep on L of the hedge away from the road (150m). Stay with the hedge when it bends R. Near the top go over the end of the raised reservoir to the next field (300m). Carry on at the R edge to the cart track (200m).

ⓔ *Extension of ¾ km/½ mile to Rhode: Turn L on the track (300m). At the end continue ahead R of the hedge (350m). Stay ahead across the next field to the protruding hedge corner (120m), up the R edge of the fields and over to the top corner at the road junction near the houses of Rhode (550m).*

ⓕ *Walk down the side lane R to the bottom (500m) ✿ and follow the bend R to Priory Farm (30m). Don't continue on the drive to the farmhouse but fork L on the track skirting L of the buildings and pass round L to the bridge over the Oakhanger Stream (100m).* ✳ ➜ ⑧

⑦ Cross the narrow field ahead to a 5-way path junction near the trees (50m). Don't go through the trees over the bridge, but turn L along the edge of the field (40m). At the bend don't continue ahead but bear R along the edge of the fields near the stream in the trees. Keep on through several fields. The stiles between them are some way out from the corners. When near Priory Farm watch out for the footbridge (1100m). Cross it and continue to the gate (200m). ✳ Turn R up the track.

⑧ Go on up through the wood to a bend at a field gate L (and an entrance R to Wick Wood which can be used for diversions or short cuts) (400m). Stay on the track eventually between fields and the malmscarp to the footpath R in the field beside the first garden (850m). *It is worth staying on the track (100m) to see Candovers, then returning. The road is used by few vehicles and offers a quick way down to the Red Lion (1500m).*

⑨ Go down the L edge of the field (150m). Near the barn exit L. Keep on in the same direction down through the wood diverging from the field (30m). Cross the track from the field and continue down in the same line to the corner of another field (350m). Follow the R edge to the bottom corner (400m).

⑩ Cross the ditch to the field ahead. Cut straight across the L corner (80m) and bear slightly L over the next field (150m). In the next follow the L edge round the corner (50m) and out to the road at Oakhanger (150m).

⑪ Walk up the road L to the **Red Lion** at the junction (500m) and ahead to the village green (300m).

24 Selborne and Noar Hill

About 7 km/4¼ miles with an extension of 3 km/2 miles; a hilly route through farmland and hangers; shady in summer; splendid views. OS maps 1:25000 133 Haslemere, 1:50000 186 Aldershot.

Start from the public car park behind the *Selborne Arms,* SU 741 335, or, on the extension, from the verge below Button's Lane, SU 739 308.

Linking walks 19★
20❖ 21◉ 22❀ 43✳

The Selborne Arms ☎ 01420 511247
The Queens Hotel ☎ 01420 511454

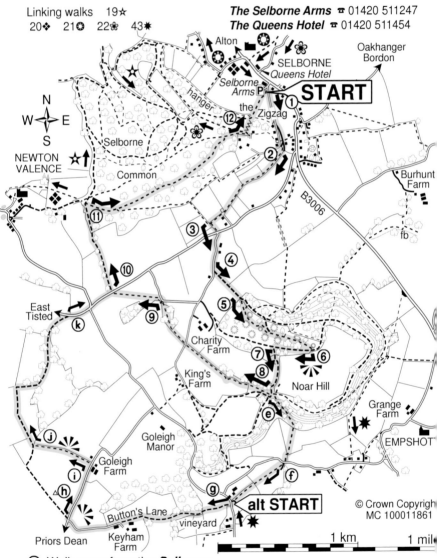

© Crown Copyright
MC 100011861

① Walk away from the **Selborne Arms** on the little road past the car park (250m). At the houses diverge L on the side track (150m).

② Fork R at the first house and immediately join the narrow footpath ahead, L of the field. Stay

48

ahead at L edge of the fields up to the next house L (600m) and the end of the next field (100m) but don't cross into the next field.

③ Turn L to the road (100m) and follow the lane opposite (250m).

④ Just before the first house R turn L up the track (300m). ✳

⑤ Just after the R field enter the nature reserve R. Keep on in the same direction, making your way up between old chalkpits, parallel with the track outside the reserve (300m). Join the track from a gate L and stay ahead to the field and seat on the top of Noar Hill (300m).

⑥ Turn R outside the field on the bridleway in the reserve (250m).

⑦ Take the first L down through the trees and between fields to the complex junction (300m).

ⓔ *Extension of 3 km/2 miles: Turn L on the bridleway and R, immediately, on the footpath down the chalk escarpment (300m). At the field, aim slightly R down past the end of the field below to the lowest point (250m).*

ⓕ *Cross the road into the field slightly R and pass through the middle to the gateway in the end hedge (250m). Carry on along the R edge of the next field and past the house to the next road (200m).*

ⓖ *Slightly L (20m) ascend the byway, Button's Lane, under the trees on the other side, past Priors Dean Vineyard (200m) to the drive from Keyham Farm (600m). Keep on up to the next road (350m). It is easier and shorter to continue on the track opposite but more interesting to go via Goleigh Farm:*

ⓗ *Walk down the road R to Goleigh Farm (400m).*

ⓘ *Just before the house L go up the edge of the field (400m).*

The altitude near the top of this field is 210m/700'. The wooded eminence, right, is Selborne Common. Left of it is the church at Newton Valence. The distant hills, right of it, are the chalk escarpment which forms the rim of the Weald - the North Downs. Further right are the radomes at Oakhanger down in their electrically-quiet bowl.

ⓙ *Join the track outside and descend R round several bends and curves to the road (1000m).*

ⓚ *Walk along the road R, past side roads R & L (150m) to the end of the field L (200m). Turn L on the path under the trees.* ➜⑩

⑧ At the complex junction take the 1st R, a footpath. Avoid joining the parallel bridleway and the track to the field L and keep on under the trees to the field ahead (150m). Follow the R edge down round a projecting corner of wood and on to the road (550m). Continue opposite along the hedge then through the trees (350m).

⑨ Carry on into the next field L of the road (20m) and cross obliquely aiming for the bottom end of the sloping hedge in the next field R (350m). Cross the road to the path almost opposite.

⑩ Keep on up the path to the wood, Selborne Common (450m) and on (200m). ❖☆

⑪ Take the 1st side path R. Avoid the diverging side path R (200m) and keep on, eventually curving L to a T-junction of paths (900m).

⑫ Turn R along the garden hedge (100m). ✿ Turn L to the stone on the brow of Selborne Hanger. Go down the Zigzag (300m) and ahead to the *Selborne Arms* (200m). ✪

25 Holybourne and Upper Froyle

About 7 km/4¼ miles; over farmland; usually good in winter. One steep climb. OS maps 1:25000 144 Basingstoke, 1:50000 186 Aldershot.

Start from Holybourne, SU 736 410; park on the main road near the *White Hart* or in Lower Neatham Mill Lane. Alternatively start from Upper Froyle, parking near the T-junction into the village, SU 753 426.

Linking walks   26✿   29✳   32✳   34✤

The White Hart   ☎ 01420 87654   **The Hen & Chicken**   ☎ 01420 22115

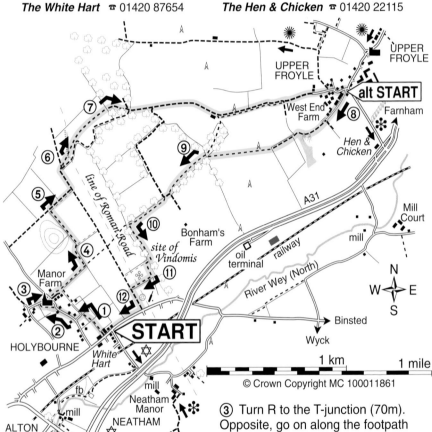

① At Holybourne take the track beside the former chapel opposite Carpenters Close. Carry on ahead through fields to the tarmac drive (200m) then L to the road (50m).

② Go R along the road past the pond (200m) and bear L across the churchyard to the next road (70m).

③ Turn R to the T-junction (70m). Opposite, go on along the footpath past the houses (100m) and ahead at the R edge of the field (250m).

④ Don't continue into the next field but go L round the corner and on beside the hedge (150m) then into the field R and on beside the same hedge over a rise and down to the cart track (300m).

⑤ Turn R down the track to the T-junction (200m) then L (150m).

50

⑥ After the bend, go up the field R, not on the bridleway at the edge, but the public footpath straight up. The Roman road protrudes half way up. On top, aim for the gate 100m L of the corner (500m).

⑦ Carry on along the cart track through the wood, down between fields then up to Upper Froyle (1500m) and along the tarmac lane, round R to the grass triangle near the village street (200m). ✳❋

⑧ At the triangle turn away from the village on the drive L of the farm buildings. Stay ahead on the track down past the pond (500m) and up to the end of the first field (200m). In the next field cross slightly R to the far corner at the wood (500m).

⑨ Stay ahead through the trees to the next large field (20m) and go down the L edge (350m). Join the farm track briefly (40m). When it bends R continue ahead at the R edge of the field (300m).

⑩ At the end go round the corner L and on beside the trees (300m).

⑪ Turn R down the bank, over the footbridge and into the field, site of the Vindomis excavation (50m). Follow the L edge (120m). At the sports field either cross diagonally to the gate or go R on the path outside it (120m) and L on the track to the road (150m).

⑫ Walk along the road R to the parking place near the **White Hart** (300m). ✿

Vindomis is the Roman name of a lost town, probably the one brought to light at Neatham and Holybourne in 1969 during the digging for the Alton by-pass. A Roman list of staging points survives, called the *Antonine Itineraries*. Iter XV puts Vindomis 15 miles from *Calleva Atrebatum* (Silchester) on the route to Winchester. The distance is correct but the direction problematic. It is not on the direct line to Winchester but on the Chichester road which branches from it. No inscribed masonry has been found to confirm the identification.

1st century bronze wire bracelet from Vindomis

actual size

The excavated town was at a crossing point on the Wey and the intersection of Roman roads from Silchester to Chichester and Winchester to Farnham, with a fifth road to the Roman pottery works at Alice Holt. The archæologists revealed only two buildings of stone but hundreds of small 1st-4th century objects were collected and the seeds of wild plants from the mud in the wells. The town occupied 35 acres/14 hectares and may have had a population of 4000. There were several industries. Fortification suggests it may have had a tax collecting role. Being on the river, it may have been a frontier post of the Atrebates, the Belgic tribe whose capital became the walled town, CALLEVA ATREBATUM (Silchester), and base of the Roman District Commissioner.

Neatham was a Saxon royal manor and it is interesting to speculate whether there may have been any Dark Age continuity from the Roman settlement.

Excavations on the Romano-British Small Town at Neatham, Hampshire 1969-1979
Martin Hill & David Graham, Hants Field Club 1983 166pp

26 Holybourne, Wyck and East Worldham

About 9 km/5¾ miles; through hop kiln country over undulating farmland .
OS maps 1:25000 144 Basingstoke, 1:50000 186 Aldershot.

Linking walks   25✿   27☆   28✴   34✹   38✳

Start from Holybourne, SU 736 411; park beside the main road or Lower
Neatham Mill Lane. Alternatively, start at East Worldham, SU 749 380, parking
in the layby on the main road or at the church.

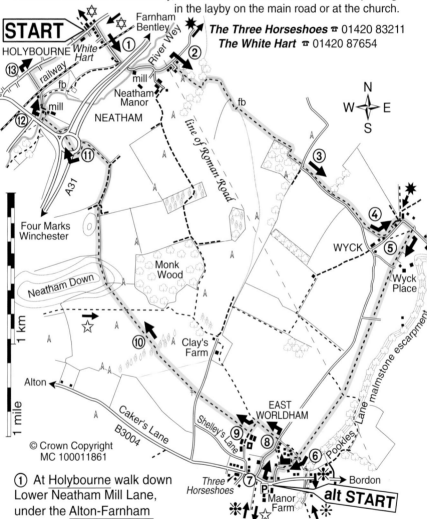

The Three Horseshoes ☎ 01420 83211
The White Hart ☎ 01420 87654

① At Holybourne walk down
Lower Neatham Mill Lane,
under the Alton-Farnham
railway line to the A31 Alton bypass
(300m). Pass under the road and
over the River Wey to the mill.
Keep on up the road, round the
bend at Neatham Manor (250m),
to the next houses (150m). ✴

② Turn into the little side road R
(50m) and follow the footpath
ahead under trees (150m). At the
field cross ahead to the tip of the
wood (70m) then turn L across to

the next group of trees (70m). Go R round the edge of the trees to the little stream then follow it across the field R to the hedge-end (300m) and on (70m). Cross the footbridge. The right-of way is a line diverging from the stream to the L corner of the wood at the top (300m) but it is sometimes easier to follow the stream to the R corner (250m) then turn L beside the wood (200m). Follow the edge of the wood under the power lines to the road (300m).

③ Cross the road and continue ahead, not on the road, but at the edge of the fields above it.

④ When the road bends away R (600m), keep to the edge of the field up round behind houses (250m). Skirt round the garden of the top house to the road bend in Wyck (100m). ✳

⑤ Take the road ahead and turn R at the footpaths (100m). Follow the L edge of the field (300m). Cross the drive of Wyck Place and go straight on along the middle of the fields between road R and the malmstone escarpment L (950m). Cross the sunken track (Pookles Lane on the Roman road), and carry on (500m). ✳

⑥ At the end, cross the boundary path and fence to East Worldham church (100m). Turn L & R out of the churchyard then walk L along the lane to the main road (200m) and R past the layby (50m). ☆

The ***Three Horseshoes*** is further down the main road (200m).

⑦ Downhill from the layby (50m), take the Wyck/Binsted road, 1st R, to the end of the houses (300m).

⑧ Opposite the shared drive, take the path L down the field (200m).

⑨ At the path junction turn L to buildings (150m) then R down the field, over the road (450m) near the electricity pole. Keep on the same line, to the trees below (400m). Take the path through the trees to the next field (80m).

⑩ Stay ahead over a cross path (200m) to the top (aim for the highest point in the field 100m L of the pylon in the saddle on the skyline) (200m). Continue ahead, always at the R edges, to the A31 Alton by-pass, (1100m) and drop L to the roundabout (100m).

⑪ Cross the roundabout (150m). Where the Farnham road leaves it cross the verge up to the fence at the end of the ditch. Follow the fence up L (40m) then go down the middle of the field (200m).

⑫ Join the path outside the field and go R to Upper Neatham Mill House (70m) then L over the River Wey and out along the drive (80m). Continue ahead up the lane into Holybourne (250m).

⑬ Walk along the main road R to the ***White Hart*** (500m) and your starting point. ✿

Oast houses are called hop kilns in Hampshire. They dot the countryside between Farnham and Selborne telling of extensive hop growing in the past. Hops must be dried immediately and the kilns operated 24 hours a day to keep pace with the hop picking in early September. Anthracite or charcoal was burned at ground level. The hops were on a grating above. The tall roof and cowl helped to draw air through. More recently ordinary sheds were used with oil burners and electric fans. One or two old hop kilns are still in working order though disused. Their use came to an end in the late 1990's.

27 East & West Worldham and Neatham Down

About 8¾ km/5½ miles with an extension of 2 km/1½ mile to Hartley Mauditt and a short cut of ¾ km/½ mile; undulating farm country on the malmstone.
OS maps 1:25000 133 Haslemere or 144 Basingstoke, 1:50000 186 Aldershot.

Start from East Worldham, SU 749 380; park in the layby on the main road. At weekends there is parking in the industrial estate, SU 727 392, off Wilsom Road, Alton. On the extension park near Hartley Mauditt Church, SU 742 361.

Linking walks   18◇   21✿   26☆   28✪   34❉   38✤

The Three Horseshoes   ☎ 01420 83211

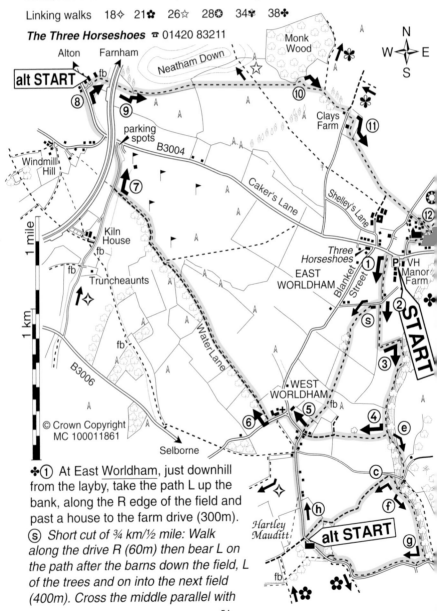

✤① At East Worldham, just downhill from the layby, take the path L up the bank, along the R edge of the field and past a house to the farm drive (300m).
Ⓢ *Short cut of ¾ km/½ mile: Walk along the drive R (60m) then bear L on the path after the barns down the field, L of the trees and on into the next field (400m). Cross the middle parallel with*

the R edge (250m). In the next, drop to the stream (100m) and go straight up the other side of the valley aiming for the house with large chimneys (200m). Join the road at the bend and turn R. ➔⑤

② Cross and go on along the R edge of the field (300m).

③ In the next field turn back L beside the hedge (200m) then R along the top of the malmscarp to the path junction halfway along the next field (700m).

ⓔ *Extension of 2 km/1½ mile: Stay ahead on the path obliquely L down the escarpment, along the top of the field, out on the track and over the road (350m). Don't continue ahead but go up steps R to the top of the hanger (80m).*

☆ ⓒ *Cut in the extension: Go R, round the end of the field (100m) then follow the track diverging from the edge over the field to the road (800m). Turn R.* ➔ⓗ

ⓕ *Carry on (L) along the top of the hanger to the edge of the cleft concealing the next road (600m).*

ⓖ *Turn R up the path above the cleft and follow the edge of the field round several curves to the end at a little wood (800m). Just round the corner R take the exit track to the road (50m)* ✿ *and follow it R past the pond (100m).*

ⓗ *From Hartley Mauditt Church stay on the road* ◇ *to the L bend in the next village (700m).* ➔⑤

④ Turn R away from the hanger on the path across the field. Keep on along the track to the houses and road (600m) ◇ then R.

⑤ Walk along the road to West Worldham Church (170m) then L past Manor Farm (120m).

⑥ Just after the barns turn R down the track. Use the path at the L edge of the fields above the ravine (1100m). In the golf course stay at the edge then pass between fields to the drive of Kiln House (750m).

⑦ Go R to the end of the drive (300m), L under the road bridge and up the main road (400m).

⑧ Just before the little industrial estate turn R along the top edge of the field, round down to and over the footbridge (200m).

⑨ Cross the dual carriageway to the field opposite (50m) and go straight on to the projecting corner of the field above (150m). Ascend into the field L but keep on in the same direction on the haggis path above the hedge (400m). Stay ahead over the next field and the crossing path (400m) ☆ to the R edge of Monk Wood (300m). ❁

⑩ Just round the tip of the wood bear R across the field to the R edge and go on down past the house, Clays Farm (400m).

⑪ Exit at the corner. Go R (30m), then L on the footpath around the next house (converted hop kiln). After the garden (100m) carry on up the fields (500m). Disregard the track R to the buildings and go up to the houses (200m). Cross the road. Go up the drive opposite (100m) then L of the houses at the R edge of the field (100m). ✪

⑫ On top of the ridge turn R on the cross path at the wall through East Worldham Churchyard (150m) then L down the lane to the main road (100m), over it and R to the village hall layby (50m).

The ***Three Horseshoes*** is 200m further down the road.

Bordon

28 East Worldham, Wyck and Oakhanger

About 9 km/5¾ miles with a short cut of 2½ km/1½ miles; over farmland, heath and woodland. The route crosses the Gault clay which is best avoided in wet seasons. OS maps 1:25000 133 Haslemere, 1:50000 186 Aldershot.

Start from the layby on the main road in East Worldham, SU 749 380. The car park on Shortheath, SU 775 369, is near the route (start clockwise round pond).

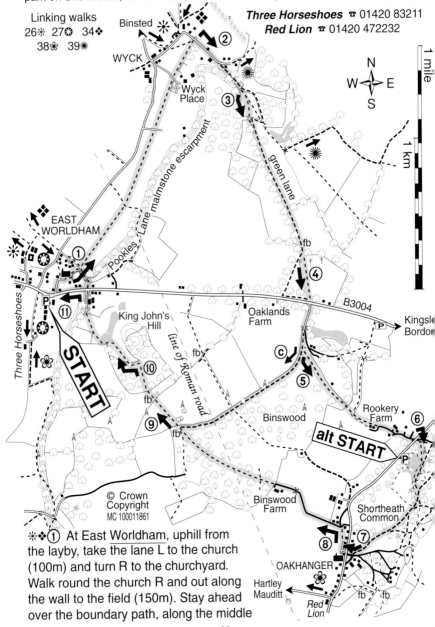

Three Horseshoes ☎ 01420 83211
Red Lion ☎ 01420 472232

Linking walks
26✳ 27✿ 34❖
38✲ 39✴

© Crown Copyright
MC 100011861

✳❖① At East Worldham, uphill from the layby, take the lane L to the church (100m) and turn R to the churchyard. Walk round the church R and out along the wall to the field (150m). Stay ahead over the boundary path, along the middle

56

of the field between the road L and malmscarp R, over a sunken track (Pookles Lane, Roman road) (500m), over a concrete farm track (500m), past the L hedge corner of Wyck Place (300m), over the drive (100m) to the road in Wyck (300m).

② Turn R along the narrow road (200m). ✳ Just after Bumbles Oasthouse, diverge R on the track down the escarpment under trees out to the fields (200m).

③ Don't continue on the bridleway but turn into the R field. Stay near the R edge down to the opening R-of-centre at the bottom (200m). From the exit track turn L into the trees to the bridleway (20m). Keep on along the belt of trees between fields (green lane) until it bends ½R just after a bridge (1000m).

④ Cross the field ahead on the same line, aiming 100m R of the house, to an exit point in the trees (300m). Go out to the road and along the tarmac drive opposite. Just over the bridge and round the bend enter the field R (which is the corner of Binswood) (250m).

ⓒ *Short cut of 2½ km/1½ miles: Follow the R edge to the trees and carry on, outside fields, to the 2nd footpath to the fields (1200m).* ➔⑨

⑤ Follow the R edge briefly (50m) but when it curves away R follow the L edge. The right of way is about 40m from the edge but eventually converges on it into the corner (500m). Keep on ahead out of Binswood. After the side path L (50m) the right of way sinks between hedges but usually there is a pleasant path at the edge of the R field. After the houses stay on the track to the road (500m).

⑥ Cross into the wood opposite. Don't follow the vehicle track but the path R of it (40m) and find the side path R to the pond (100m). Take the wide path L of the pond until it joins the track (200m) and continue (R) to the village green at Oakhanger (600m). ❀ (The **Red Lion** is L along the road (300m).)

⑦ Just R of the church pass between the houses (30m). Follow the service road R behind the houses and continue on the path to the next track (150m).

⑧ Turn L along the track between fields to Binswood Farm (600m). From the end of the track keep on, always ahead, through Binswood. The path is often obscure (800m).

⑨ Near the (NW) corner of the wood exit over the footbridge and cross the fields aiming slightly L of the top of King John's Hill (300m). Ascend through the wood (200m).

⑩ At the field turn L along the edge of the wood (100m) then R into the field. Follow the line of trees over the shoulder of the hill then aim L of the ponds (200m). After the ponds go ½R up the next field past the protruding corner of another field L to the tarmac farm drive (200m). Go R, past the barn, up to the road in East Worldham (150m). Cross to the pavement.

⑪ The parking layby is L up the road (250m). To continue off-road, go on through the grounds of Old School House up to the field (40m). Cross the L corner up to the next field (30m) and go up the L edge to the cross path near the church (100m). Go though the churchyard L to the lane (150m) and L to the road (100m). ✪

29 Upper Froyle and Yarnhams

About 8½ km/5¼ miles with a slightly shorter alternative section. A tranquil route over undulating farmland with fine views. OS maps 1:25000 144 Basingstoke, 1:50000 186 Aldershot.

Start from a roadside parking place near the road junction at the SW end of Upper Froyle, SU 753 426. Fairly near the route there is a large layby on the A31, SU 760 427, and parking opposite Lower Froyle village hall, SU 760 441.

Linking 25✳ 30❖ 32☆ 35✲ 36❀   ***The Hen & Chicken*** ☎ 01420 22115

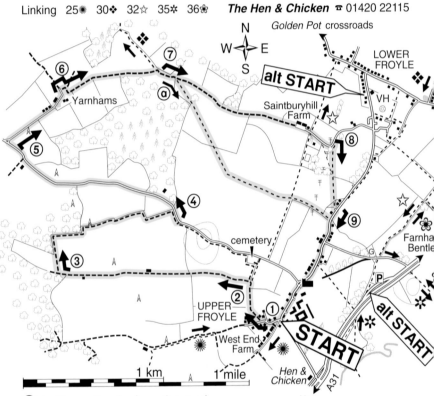

© Crown Copyright MC 100011861

① In Upper Froyle, from the road junction follow the tarmac lane round R past the houses (150m). After the small side road turn R on the cart track past a house and round R between fields (300m).

② Stay on the track (permissive) round the L bend, over a rise and past barns to the wood L (1400m).

③ Just after the start of the wood (70m), turn R up the field R to the hedge bend at trees (permissive path). Carry on up beside the hedge to the top (300m) then follow the edge R round several bends to the road access in the dip (1100m).

④ Walk up the road L. Pass the house R at the wood (200m) and another house L (1000m) to the Yarnhams tarmac drive R (200m).

⑤ Turn R to Yarnhams (500m).

⑥ After the farm buildings and the big house, just round the L bend (20m), turn R on the cart track, R again, then L (50m). Go on along the track beside the fields to the R bend with side path L (700m). ❖ Go on round the bend watching out for a footpath to the field R (120m). ⓐ *Slightly shorter alternative: Take the path R through the trees diagonally down the small field (200m) and on in the same oblique line in the next field through the middle of the bottom hedge (300m) to the valley bottom (200m). Go L along the valley bottom, over a cross path at the corner of a field (500m) and on beside the hedge to the road (300m).* ➧ⓨ

⑦ Stay on the track along the hilltop, eventually down to the farm (1000m).☆ At the lane, keep on to the next house & garden R (100m) and a bit further (100m).

⑧ Just round the bend, climb the path up the R bank and cross the fields. The right of way starts 100m L of the garden hedge but diverges to the gap in the trees on the brow. Keep on down to the houses and out through a garden (400m). ✳❀

⑨ Go R on the road, past a lane R, opposite Froyle Church and the manor house L (500m) to the next road junction (300m). ✳

The Domesday Book entry for Froyle
actual size

HAMPSHIRE
XIIII   LAND OF ST MARY'S OF WINCHESTER
Itself the abbey holds <u>FROLI</u>. Always it was there. TRE   <u>In NEATHAM Hundred</u> it was rated for x hides; now for viii hides. Land for x ploughs. In demesne are iii ploughs; xv villeins & xxiii bordars with viii ploughs. There is a church; x serfs; ii mills @ xxii shillings & vi pence; viii acres pasture.
TRE and later value £xii; Now £xv. However it renders £xx of revenue.

The Domesday Book was compiled in 1086 by order of William the Conqueror. Originally it was loose folios but by 1200 these had been sewn together to form a book which was then entitled *LIBER DE WINTONIA*, the Book of Winchester. The national treasury resided at Winchester until it moved to Whitehall in the 13th century and the book was an estimate of tax. Entries were in two columns on both sides of the parchment, 15" x 11" (approx A3), in county sections then in order of ownership by size. The name *Domesday* appears in court records in the 13th century but was probably satirical at first; this was the first exercise in red tape on a national scale. The book is on display at the National Archives in Kew.

30 Lower Froyle and Frog Lane (and Well)

About 9½ km/6 miles with an extension of ¾ km/½ mile; undulating farmland and woods. OS maps 1:25000 144 Basingstoke, 1:50000 186 Aldershot.

Start from Lower Froyle, parking at the roadside opposite the village hall, SU 760 441. On the extension, park at Well opposite the pub, SU 760 466.

Linking walks   29❖   31✿   32✣
35✳   36◇   2◆   3❁

The Chequers ☎ 01256 862605
The Anchor ☎ 01420 23261

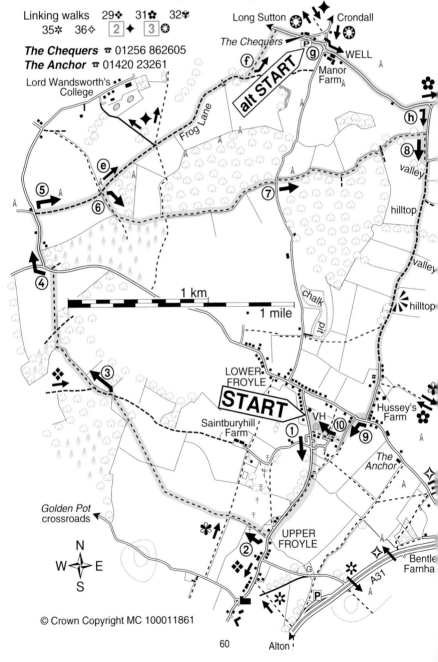

© Crown Copyright MC 100011861

60

① From the village hall at Lower Froyle walk up the road over the hill (400m). After the house on top take the path under trees L of the road and re-join the road down to the 1st field R in the dip (500m). ❖

② Turn R on the track outside the garden. Go on through the field, over a cross path at the end of the L field (300m) and along the valley until level with a hedge descending the R valleyside (500m). Bear R to the middle of the bottom hedge of the field (200m) then rise obliquely up to the top corner, cutting through the trees before the top (550m).

③ At the top turn L on the track. When it bends ½L (150m) stay at the R edge of the field ahead into the wood (400m). Bear R down the clearing into the corner of the next field (100m). Over the track, go up the R edge of the field to the top corner of the wood (100m) then straight on over the field. Aim just R of the end of the wood over the ridge to join the road just R of a track in the wood opposite (250m).

④ Walk up the road L (80m) and R up the side road over the ridge past a house R (150m) and down to a side road L (200m).

⑤ Opposite the side road, turn R on Frog Lane, a track between fields, to the corner of the wood. There is sometimes a path with better views in the L field (500m).

ⓔ *Extension of ¾ km/½ mile: Continue on Frog Lane past a side track L at footpaths L & R (500m)* ✦ *and round curves L & R to a group of three field openings (600m). Keep on ahead but watch out for access to the field L just round a slight L bend into a dip (200m).*

ⓕ *In the field ascend ½R over the highest point to the road (400m) and turn R to the **Chequers** in Well (250m).* ✪

ⓖ *After the pub stay on the larger road to the well at the staggered crossroads (100m) and ahead past Manor Farm R (850m).* ✿

ⓗ *Turn R down the next side road to the side track R (200m).* ➔⑧

⑥ Turn R on the cross path up through the edge of the wood (200m). After the corner of the R field follow the path round L, soon beside another field L.

> The parallel Chalk ridge far L is the continuation of the North Downs from the Hog's Back in Surrey. Over it, Lord Wandsworths College is visible and further away Odiham Airfield (RAF) from which fly the Chinooks that are usually exercising overhead.

At the cross path (350m) stay ahead on the path in the wood, beside fields R, to the road (800m).

⑦ Cross slightly L (10m) and carry on along the path at the edge of the wood in a slight valley (900m). Continue up to the road (250m). ✿ and descend R to the bend (150m).

⑧ Go down the path in the trees R of the road (200m). When the road bends L stay ahead up the cart track between fields. The track crosses a ridge to a valley (600m) then another ridge with a fine picnic spot (350m). Stay ahead at tarmac (450m) ✸ to the T-junction at the pond in Lower Froyle (400m). ✸✧

⑨ Turn R along the road (100m) then L along Park Lane to the end garden (200m).

⑩ Turn R at the garden to the playing field (100m) and cross obliquely to the village hall (150m).

31 Bentley to Montgomery's Farm

Short version from Bentley Church about 7¾ km/5 miles or long version via the village, 9½ km/6 miles; through farming country over the chalk ridge; a good winter walk. OS maps 1:25000 144 Basingstoke, 1:50000 186 Aldershot.

For the short version start at Bentley Church (not Sundays), SU 784 446; for the longer at Bentley recreation ground car park, SU 783 439 or the village street.

Linking walks
30✿ 32✪ 33✦ 5✳ 12◈

The Star ☎ 01420 23184

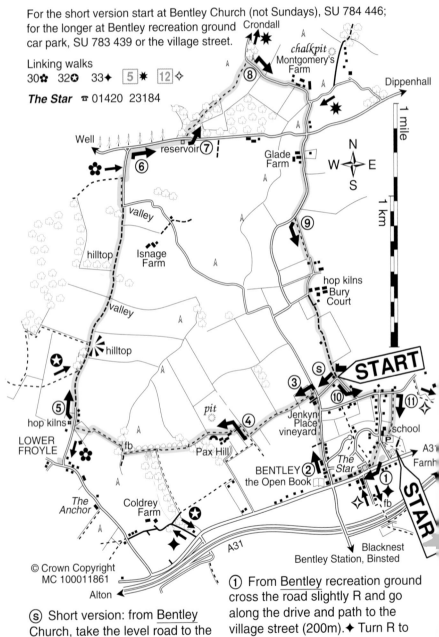

① From Bentley recreation ground cross the road slightly R and go along the drive and path to the village street (200m).✦ Turn R to the crossroads (250m).

Ⓢ Short version: from Bentley Church, take the level road to the end at Jenkyn Place (200m). ✦③

② Go past the crossroads to see the Open Book R then return to the crossroads and walk up the minor road beside the Memorial Hall (300m). Join the footpath L of the road, up to Jenkyn Place (300m).

③ Just up the road from Jenkyn Place (20m) turn L into the drive Stay ahead beside the garden wall and vineyard into the field before the house, Pax Hill (500m). ✪

④ Skirt R round the field (200m). Watch out for a gap in the hedge R near the garden and continue on the other side and through the next field (350m). At the corner cross the hedge L but resume the original direction beside the belt of trees to the R corner of the wood (200m). Stay ahead between the wood and the belt of trees (350m). Go round the next corner then cross into the next field and follow the edge as before (250m). At the next hedge bend, enter the adjacent field L. Turn R but diverge from the hedge to the exit, L of converted hop kilns (oast houses) (100m). ✿

⑤ Walk up the road R (150m). Stay ahead up the track over the hilltop (picnic spot)(400m), down through the valley (300m) and over another rise to the road (600m). Go up the path L of the road (200m) then up the road to the end (200m).

⑥ Turn R up the larger road (on the North Downs chalk ridge) to the highest point (400m).

⑦ Just after the hump (reservoir) with a clump of trees in the field R, take the footpath L through the wood and down between fields to the next road (700m). ✳

⑧ Walk up the winding road R past Montgomery's Farm (350m) and a side road L (200m) to the crossroads (200m). Cross and carry on down through the dip (300m) and over the rise. Watch out for a path L beside a downhill hedge where the road swings R across the flank of the hill (300m).

⑨ Go down the footpath R of the hedge (300m) then follow the estate road up round to the main entrance of Bury Court (250m). Stay ahead on the track over the rise to Bentley Church (600m).

⑩ Take the downhill road (200m) and turn L at the T-junction. Go on past the side road R and the Old Parsonage (where Jane Austen's brother lived) to the start of the first field R (250m). ✧

⑪ Follow the path along the edge of the field, past the school (300m), to the recreation ground (100m).

Buzzards look like rooks in flight and are more likely to be noticed when soaring. They have broad wings and a broad tail with convex end. The country round about, wheat fields and woods, is also suitable for kites and they are increasingly visiting the area. They have chevron tails and longer narrow wings with obvious pale patches and, being gregarious, may gyrate in numbers.

32 The Froyles and Coldrey

About 8½ km/5¼ miles over rolling farmland. An extension of 1½ km/1 mile to Isington and short cut of 1 km/¾ mile can be used together; good in winter; not much shade. OS maps 1:25000 144 Basingstoke, 1:50000 186 Aldershot.

Start from the A31 layby, SU 760 427. There are a few roadside parking spots in Upper Froyle and opposite the village hall Lower Froyle.

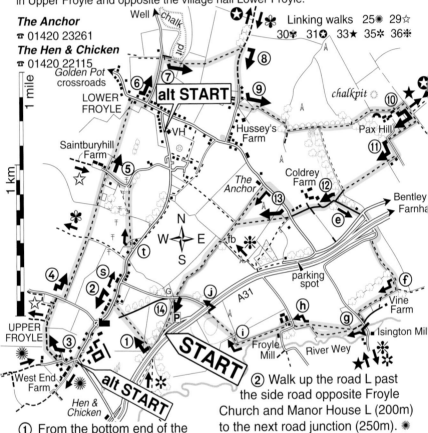

The Anchor
☎ 01420 23261
The Hen & Chicken
☎ 01420 22115

Linking walks 25❋ 29☆ 30❀ 31◉ 33★ 35❋ 36❋

① From the bottom end of the layby, walk along the verge of the A31 (70m) then enter the field R. Go straight up the field over a drive and on into Upper Froyle (400m).

ⓢ *Short cut of 1 km/¾ mile: Walk down the road to the valley (300m).*

ⓣ *After the dip (80m) find the path between the houses L and go up the fields to the lane over the top (400m). Turn L up the lane past the house L (200m) and into the field R beside the next garden.* ➔⑤

② Walk up the road L past the side road opposite Froyle Church and Manor House L (200m) to the next road junction (250m). ❋

③ Follow the smaller road round R past the houses (150m). After the little side road R take the cart track R past a house and round R between fields (300m). ☆ Don't go round the L bend but stay ahead down to the cemetery gate (200m).

④ Go R on the lane (70m), L down the field beside the hedge to the valley track (450m), ❀ straight up the fields ahead and over the lane into the field opposite (450m).

⑤ Go straight down through the fields to the bottom L corner and out between houses to the road in Lower Froyle (400m).

⑥ Walk R along the road (100m) and up the side road, first L (300m).

⑦ Turn R into the drive of Froyle chalkpit and R into the field. Go up the L edge (100m), into the next field, over the shoulder of the ridge then, slightly L, down to the R end of the little wood (500m). ❂

⑧ Walk down the track R and on along the tarmac lane (400m).

⑨ Turn L into the field after the hop kiln houses R and cross to the far L corner (100m). Go round the hedge bend into the adjacent field and follow the hedge R to the end (250m). In the next field go R & L round the corner behind the belt of trees (30m) (not up the farm track) and keep on along the fence & ditch (200m). At the end of the R trees cross to the adjacent field R but keep on in the same direction at the top edge (200m). At the large trees go through to the L field and carry on now at R edges (350m).

⑩ Just after Pax Hill (buildings R) go through the gap R but keep on beside the hedge (80m) and round the corner (100m). Avoid the side path L. ★ Soon after it (50m) turn R alongside the large field to the Pax Hill drive (250m).

⑪ Walk down the drive L (120m) and R into the field at the houses. Follow the path past the gardens then stay ahead over the field and out on the track in the trees to the T-junction below Coldrey (550m). ✳

ⓔ *Extension of 1½ km/1 mile via Isington Mill: Go down the track L, under the A31, up the other side,* *round the bend (350m) then down the R edge of the field (400m).*

ⓕ *Near the bottom cross to the R field. Go round the next corner R (50m), up the L edge to the road (350m) then L to the drive (70m).*

ⓖ *The route is along the track opposite but cross the River Wey to see Isington Mill then return (150m) and take the track into the field (100m). Make for the top corner of the hedge ahead and follow it to the next road (400m).*

ⓗ *On the other side, just above the house (20m), turn L into the barnyard, L to the path above the the valley and R along it (400m).*

ⓘ *At the end of the hedge go up between the fields above (100m) then aim over the R slope of the hillock, to the top fence 150m from the R corner (300m).*

ⓙ *Cross the A31 to the lane opposite (round central barrier R) (50m) and walk down to the end of the first field L (250m). Turn L ➜⑭*

⑫ Go up the track R past the houses R to the road (350m).

⑬ In wet seasons walk along the road R to the **Anchor** and take the path in the field L of the pub (300m), but, when dry, pass through the wall opposite and cross the fields obliquely to the 4-way junction at the hedge & ditch after the power lines (400m). Follow the hedge & ditch to the end (150m). Cross the ditch R under the trees and go on in the same direction at the edge of the field (550m). ✳ Cross the road.

⑭ Go along the R edge of the field (but before that turn R to see the gas regulation station). At the end of the field stay ahead on the path through trees to the layby (300m).

33 Isington and Bentley

About 8½ km/5¼ miles over rolling farm country; little shade; many stiles; sticky mud in winter. OS maps: 1:25000 144 Basingstoke, 1:50000 186 Aldershot.

Start at Bentley recreation ground car park, SU 787 442, or the village street.

Linking walks 31✦ 32★
35❀ 36✿ 37✳ 41✪ 12❖

The Star ☎ 01420 23184

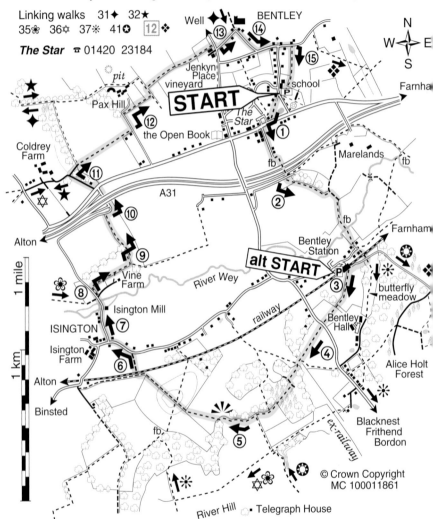

© Crown Copyright
MC 100011861

① From Bentley recreation ground cross the road slightly R and go along the drive then the path to the village street (200m). Follow the pavement R (80m). Cross the main road and take the lane beside the warehouses to the A31 (250m). Cross the footbridge.

② Follow the drive away from the sewage works gate (40m) then cross the small field L to the corner (80m). Go on round the L edge of the next field (300m) then R down between the fields to the River Wey (300m). Go straight up the meadow on the other side and out between the houses (150m). Don't turn to the road but stay ahead and cross the railway lines (Alton-Farnham) (100m). ☀☥ At the gate of the butterfly meadow, turn R to the S platform of Bentley Station (100m).

③ Along the platform (30m) take the path up the R edge of the field over the top. Go straight down the next field to the road (400m) and into the field opposite.

④ Look ahead to the corner of the hillside wood, just beyond the trees lining the R edge. The right-of-way is direct to that corner (300m) but the path is sometimes at the edge. Ascend through the wood, round L and R bends, to the field (300m). Continue at the R edge over the top to the next field (200m). ✿

⑤ Carry on down the edge above the malmscarp to the bottom of the tongue of field (Telegraph House visible back L over the hill) (300m). Go down the next field, converging on the L edge (250m). Stay ahead at the edge over the hillock and down to the railway (350m).

⑥ Go under the bridge, up to the road (150m) and L to the side road in Isington. *(If the bridge is flooded, take the track L beside the railway (400m) and turn R along the road to the 2nd side road L (300m).)*

⑦ Follow the side road down past Isington Mill and over the River Wey to the drive R (300m).

⑧ Take the path on the R bank of the road (70m) and turn R at the edge of the field to the end (300m).

⑨ Disregard the stile in the corner and turn L towards the next corner (50m), then cross into the field R and continue up the haggis path at the L edge to the road (300m).

⑩ Go R under the A31(100m). At the end, cross the road slightly L (30m) and walk up the track towards Coldrey Farm (200m). ★✦

⑪ At the bend below the large house, turn R on the track over the dam of the pond up to the field (100m). Go straight over (Telegraph House on River Hill distant R) past the houses and out (400m).

⑫ Turn L up the drive of Pax Hill (100m). Just before the bend turn R on the path along the top of the field (200m). In the next field turn L (50m) and R up to the next field, above the hedge. Stay ahead past the vineyard R and garden wall to the road at Bentley (500m).

⑬ Slightly R, opposite the gate of Jenkyn Place, follow the side road to Bentley Church (250m).

⑭ From the church take the down-hill road to the T-junction (250m) and turn L. Carry on past the side road R and the Old Parsonage R to the first field R (250m) . ❖

⑮ Take the path R along the edge to the recreation ground (300m).

Baden Powell, Robert Stephenson Smyth, Lord ,1857-1941, lived at Pax Hill until 1938. He was so competent, he became an army subaltern in India directly from Charterhouse; and by 43 he was a general. He is credited with introducing observation balloons (in Bechuanaland and Sudan) but it was withstanding the 217 day siege of Mafeking in the Boer War that brought him fame. He wrote *Aids to Scouting* for the army when he commanded the 5th Dragoon Guards in India. This led to a cult of dress and activities which turned into the Boy Scout movement. B-P retired from the army in 1910 for the full-time role of Chief Scout. He lived in Kenya for his last three years.

34 Neatham, Wyck and Binsted

About 10 km/6¼ miles with a short cut of 2½ km/1½ miles and a little extension into Binsted; rolling malmstone country dotted with hop kilns; bad mud in wet seasons. OS maps 1:25000 144 Basingstoke, 1:50000 186 Aldershot.

Start from Holybourne; park down Lower Neatham Mill Lane, SU 738 408. On the extension park in Binsted beside the village street or in the recreation ground car cark, SU 773 410 (entrance drive opposite the *The Cedars*).

Linking walks 25❅ 26✳ 27❉ 28❖ 35❆ 36◆ 37✪ 39★ 40★

The Cedars ☎ 01420 22112
The Hen & Chicken ☎ 01420 22115

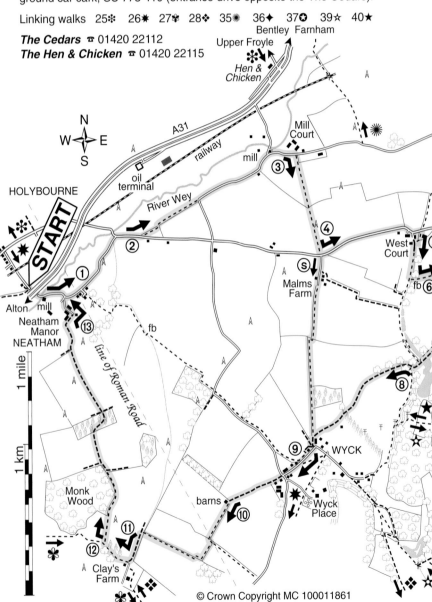

✳①　From the bottom of Lower Neatham Mill Lane go under the A31, over the River Wey and past the mill up the lane. Stay on this lane down to the junction (800m).

②　Turn R up the road (150m). Near the top enter the field L and diverge from the road, R of the hedge (100m). Stay ahead L of the hedge to the road (Alton-Farnham railway and oil terminal, below L) (400m). Keep on down past Fulling Mill Cottage, to the river bridge at the gates of Mill Court (700m). Go back to the road junction (50m) then L up the road until opposite Mill Court (200m). ✳

③　Before the next house L, go up the track R and straight over the fields to the road (700m).

Ⓢ　*Short cut of 2½ km/1½ miles: Cross the road and stay ahead on the drive to Malms Farm (200m), along the R edge of the fields (700m), up through the end of the wood (150m), through more field (200m) and along the track to the road at Wyck (80m).*✳ ✦→⑨

④　Walk L along the road to the drive of West Court (700m). ✦

⑤　Soon after the drive (40m) take the path R behind the hop kilns and down the valley under trees. Watch out for a side path L (300m).

⑥　Turn L across the brook and up to the fields. Go over to the hedge (300m), R & L round the corner (20m) and on to Binsted Church. Monty's grave is at the start of the churchyard. Follow the path R of the church to the gate (300m). ★✪

ⓔ　*Extension of ¾ km/½ mile into the village. Carry on over the road ahead between fields to the street (200m). The Cedars is R (100m).*

ⓕ　*From **The Cedars**, walk down through the village (300m) then L up from the crossroads (200m).*

⑦　From the church gate go round the bends in the lane away from the village (200m). Take the first side lane R down to the end house (300m) and pass on down the track. When this becomes private (100m) branch off R on the track in the trees. At the pond, when the track is boggy, people go along the L field or above in the trees (400m).

⑧　Go round the R bend. Disregard the stepped path L. ☆ Stay on the track up through trees then across the fields over the top, all the way to the road at Wyck (1000m).✳

⑨　Walk along the lane R to the T-junction (300m) and ahead on the track opposite (400m).

⑩　Bear L past the barns along the edge of the first field. Skirt the top edge in the 2nd (500m) and go down the R edge in the 3rd (450m).

⑪　At the bottom turn L (200m). Don't go out to the lane ✳ but follow the track R round the corner, past the house and up (250m).

⑫　Almost under the power cables turn R across the bulge in the field to the R corner of Monk Wood (200m). Go straight on R of the wood and over the fields, past numerous side tracks (1400m).

⑬　At Manor Farm turn R & L past the barns and go out along the drive of Neatham Manor (250m). ✳ Walk down the lane and under the A31 (300m) to Holybourne.

alt START

The Cedars

Blacknest

P

BINSTED

35 Binsted and Mill Court

About 8¾ km/5½ miles over undulating farmland in malmstone and hop kiln country. OS maps 1:25000 144 Basingstoke, 1:50000 186 Aldershot.

Start from the large layby on the A31, NE of the *Hen & Chicken*, SU 760 427, or from Binsted recreation ground, SU 773 410 (entrance drive opposite the pub).

Linking walks 29✲ 30✲ 32✲ 33✿
34✺ 32✲ 36✪ 37✿ 40✤

The Cedars 01420 22112
Hen & Chicken 01420 22115

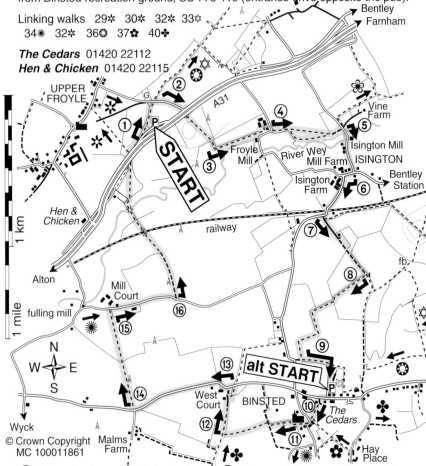

① Near the low end of the layby take the footpath through the trees (100m) and along the L edge of the field to the road (200m). ✪✿

② Turn R on the road (past two oil pipeline signs) to the A31 (300m). Look across for the stile under the trees opposite and get there round the end of the central barrier (50m). In the field aim over the L slope of the rise for the far L corner (250m).

③ Descend between the next two fields (100m) then go L below the hedge along the brow of the Wey Valley and out through the barnyard to the road (400m).

④ At the bend in the road (20m) enter the field opposite the house. Follow the R hedge until it bends R (100m) then make for the bottom of the end hedge. Carry on along the track to the next road (450m).

70

⑤ Turn R across the River Wey to Isington Mill and stay on the road up to the T-junction (300m).

⑥ Turn R. Follow the road round the L bend at the side lane (100m) and over the railway bridge (300m).

⑦ At the bend turn L on the track to the house (200m). Stay ahead up beside the wood (300m). ✿

⑧ Turn R along the (treeless) hedge in the next field (300m). At the end turn L&R to the next field and continue in the same direction (200m). Go round the corner L and on (150m). After the line of trees, turn R between fields (150m) then L to the track from the road (120m).

⑨ Turn L along the tree-lined edge then R into the sports field (200m). Cross to the car park and go down the drive into Binsted (200m). ❖

⑩ From the *Cedars* walk down the road (100m) then L on the path between houses and small fields to the next road (200m). ✳

⑪ Cross to the churchyard. Go L of the church and along the R edge to Monty's grave (200m). Keep on along the hedge (100m), R round the end (20m) then L over the field into the wooded valley (300m).

⑫ Cross the stream and turn R up the valley. Just before the hop kilns at West Court, bear R on the side path to the road (350m).

⑬ Go L along the road to the first side lane L (to Malms Farm)(700m).

⑭ Opposite the lane climb the road bank R and go past the pylon straight over the fields to the next road opposite Mill Court (700m).

⑮ Walk up the road R (500m).

⑯ At the top, just after the power cables, take the track down L past a pylon. Keep on down to pass under the railway bridge (450m). Continue ahead across the narrow fields (200m), over the footbridge, up the slope (30m) round a R bend, obliquely up below the wall to the field (30m). Aim diagonally over the top for the furthest corner. Keep on to the end between the trees (250m). ✳ Cross the dual carriageway and walk along the verge R to the layby (100m).

Hops  The hop plant, *Humulus lupulus*, has many cultivars but also grows wild, climbing in hedges. Hops are cone-like heads of female flowers. When picked, they are sticky because the bracts secrete humulin, a complex of resins and volatile oils which give bitterness and aroma to beer. The α-acids of the resins inhibit Gram positive bacteria and yeasts which spoil beer but advances in technology have made the preservative role unimportant.

Mr Bignell brought hops to Farnham in 1597. In 1870 there were 72,000 acres in 53 counties as far north as Aberdeen. By 1995 only 7630 acres/3088 ha still grew. In that year, between Bentley and Worldham, Hampshire's last three hop farmers had 146 acres but production for breweries had ceased by 2004. Hop kilns still dot the countryside. Under the Hogs Back at Puttenham is Surrey's last field of 12 acres/5 ha. Yield is about 30 zentners per acre (zentner= 50 kg). About half of English hops become pellets, vacuum packed and cold stored for uniformity. A quarter are turned into hop extract; liquid carbon dioxide is the solvent used to elute the resins and aromatic oils. The rest are used whole in the traditional manner. A few are used for pub decoration and soporific pillows.

36 Binsted, Coldrey and Isington

About 8¾ km/5½ miles with an extension of 1¼ km/¾ mile and a short cut of 2 km/1¼ mile; over undulating arable country with long views; not much shade. OS maps 1:25000 144 Basingstoke, 1:50000 186 Aldershot.

Start from Binsted recreation ground, SU 773 410, (entrance opposite the pub) or the layby on the A31 NE of the *Hen & Chicken*, SU 760 427.

Linking walks 29❀ 30◇ 32❇ 33❀ 34✦ 35✿ 37✿ 40♣

The Anchor
☎ 01420 23261
The Cedars
☎ 01420 22112
The Hen & Chicken
☎ 01420 22115

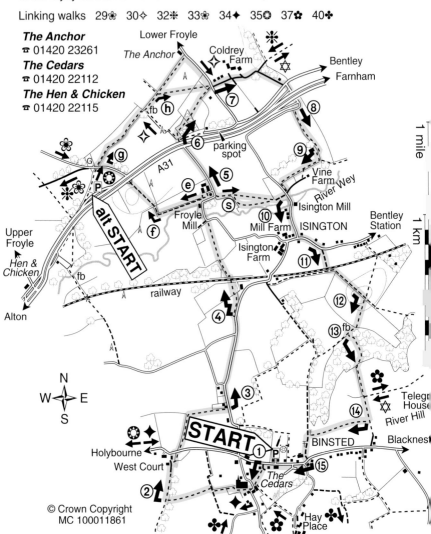

© Crown Copyright
MC 100011861

✦① At Binsted walk down the street from the *Cedars* (100m). Turn L between the houses and go on between fields to the next road (200m). Take the path through the churchyard to the end near Monty's grave (200m) and continue along the hedge (100m) Turn R at the track (20m) then L over the field into the wooded valley (300m).

② Cross the stream and go R up the valley. Just before the hop kilns at West Court bear R to the road (350m). ❍ Cross into the opposite field and follow the L hedge to the corner (250m). Turn R to the next road past the end house (300m).

③ Go L on the road, down past the second side road L (550m).

④ After it (100m), at a slight bend, climb into the field L. Follow the hedge above the road. Just round the corner go straight over the next field and railway. Stay ahead down the edge of the wood, over the next field to the gate (700m), along the road, over the River Wey and up past Froyle Mill to the farm (200m).

Ⓢ *Short cut of 2 km/1¼ mile: Turn R along the field edge (100m), then cross to the bottom corner and go on to the road (450m).* →⑩

Ⓔ *Extension of 1¼ km/¾ mile: Turn L into the barnyard, L to the path above the valley and R along it to the end of the hedge (400m).*

Ⓕ *Go up between fences to the top field (100m). Aim obliquely over the rise to the top fence 150m from the R corner (300m). Cross the A31 to the lane opposite (R of the central barrier) (50m) and go down past oil pipeline signs R to the gas regulation station (250m).* ❋❈

Ⓖ *In the R field just before the gas regulation site, take the path L of the fence to the end (600m). Cross the ditch R under trees but keep on in the same direction, R of the hedge, to a cross path (150m).*

Ⓗ *Either bear R obliquely over the fields to the corner at the wall and cross the road (400m) or stay ahead to the **Anchor** then go R along the road (300m) then L.* →⑦

⑤ Stay on the road (400m).

⑥ Slightly L (20m) cross the dual carriageway and find the access to the field behind the trees. ✧ Bear R and pass through the plantation (200m). Carry on over the large field to the protruding corner (100m) and ahead along the R edge of the smaller fields to the wall and road (100m). Cross.

⑦ Go along the drive in front of the houses to Coldrey Farm. ✿ Don't turn R before the large house but go on below the garden then bear R down to the road (350m). Pass under the A31 and up round the other side (100m).

⑧ In the field L follow the Haggis path down the R edge (400m).

⑨ Near the bottom cross into the field R. Go round the next corner R (50m) and along the L edge to the end (350m). Turn L along the road bank (70m) then join the road.

⑩ Cross the River Wey and keep on past Isington Mill, up to the T-junction (300m). Turn L along the road (200m).

⑪ Opposite the house on the bend take the track R down under the railway (Alton-Farnham)(150m) then bear L into the next field (50m) and R up the edge (250m).

⑫ At the path junction on top, turn R and descend to the corner of the wood (200m).

⑬ Keep on over the brook, along the edge of the wood (50m) then L through the wood (200m) and up the R edge of the field (400m) ❀❖ (see Telegraph House far L).

⑭ Near the top turn R on the path along the ridge to the track (450m).

⑮ Go L to the road (150m) then R into Binsted (250m).

37 Binsted and Blacknest

About 7¾ km/4¾ miles with an extension and short cut, each of 1½ km/1 mile; hilly; long views. OS maps 1:25000 144 Basingstoke, 1:50000 186 Aldershot.

Start from Binsted recreation ground car park, SU 773 410 (entrance drive opposite the *Cedars*) or park in the village street near the *Cedars*.

Linking walks   33✳   34❂   35✿   36✿   40✳   41✳

The Jolly Farmer ☎ 01420 22244
The Cedars ☎ 01420 22112

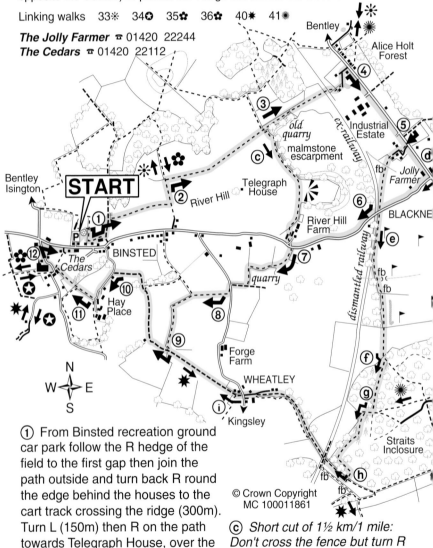

© Crown Copyright
MC 100011861

① From Binsted recreation ground car park follow the R hedge of the field to the first gap then join the path outside and turn back R round the edge behind the houses to the cart track crossing the ridge (300m). Turn L (150m) then R on the path towards <u>Telegraph House</u>, over the fields to the next track (450m). ✳
② Turn L down to the start of the hedge (150m) then R on the footpath along the side of the ridge to the trees at the far end (800m).

ⓒ *Short cut of 1½ km/1 mile: Don't cross the fence but turn R on the path along the top edge of the* <u>malmscarp</u> *and stay ahead. After the stables above River Hill Farm descend to the road at the farm drive (900m).* ➔⑦

74

③ Cross the fence ahead and go down the fields to the cutting of the dismantled <u>Bordon Railway</u> at the bottom (500m). Cross the next field obliquely R to the corner (50m) and go on outside the field to the farm track (50m). Walk up the track L to the road (150m). ✳

④ Follow the road R to Blacknest (550m). After the tarmac drive R at the start of the houses there is a track to the next houses R (100m).

ⓓ *Detour to the* **Jolly Farmer**: *Stay on the road to the pub (300m) then turn R on the Binsted road up to the top corner of the golf course L (450m).* ➤ⓔ *L or* ➤⑥ *ahead*

⑤ Enter the garden R of the track and go L round the edge to the next gate (100m). Outside follow the track round the bend to the end house. Walk along the garden path past the front door to the fields behind (100m). Aim, via the footbridge, for the top L corner by the wood and join the road (300m).

ⓔ *Extension of 1½ km/1 mile, boggy when wet: Follow the path from the road along the top edge of the golf course (800m). At the end go straight over the field (200m).*

ⓕ *Just into the wood (part of* <u>Alice Holt</u> *forest), fork R along the path in the fire-break to the next intersection of fire-breaks (400m).*

ⓖ *Turn R (30m) then continue in the original direction near the edge of the wood (400m) and round the L bend (150m). At the end turn R out of the wood (40m).* ✳

ⓗ *In the narrow field turn R along the edge of the wood (200m). At the top of the field, cross the track on the dismantled Bordon Railway and go up the bridleway between the fields (150m). Enter the field L and follow the R edge up to the hop kiln house at Wheatley (600m). Join the track to the road (70m).*

ⓘ *Continue on the track opposite round a R bend at the houses and straight over the field (600m).* ➤⑨

⑥ Walk up the road to the drive of River Hill Farm R (650m).

⑦ Go up into the field opposite the drive. Follow the bank round R and cross the end of it to enter the corner of the next field (200m). Go on along the edge of the disused quarry to the next field (200m), then L to the cart track (100m) and out R to the road (100m).

⑧ Turn L on the road but almost immediately (40m) diverge R up into the field (60m) and turn R across the middle (250m). At the far side, disregard a branch path R and bear L at the R edge (200m). Go round a corner and on (300m). At the furthest corner turn L briefly (20m). Turn back R on the cart track outside.

⑨ Stay on the track down to the malmstone barn (150m), round the bend over a ravine (350m) and L up to Hay Lane (250m).

⑩ Turn L along the lane, past Hay Place, towards the farm (200m).

⑪ Turn R on the path up the edge of the field, opposite the first farm buildings, and keep on in a straight line to <u>Binsted</u> (400m). ✚✿✪ See the church and <u>Monty</u>'s grave at the far end of the path through the churchyard, then return.

⑫ Go on along the road to the crossroads (200m) and turn R up the village street to the Recreation Ground drive L, opposite the **Cedars** (200m).

38 Oakhanger and the malmstone escarpment

About 9 km/5½ miles. An extension of 2 km/1¼ miles involves the ascent of the cliff-like escarpment which is dangerous especially when wet. Farmland and wood; undulating. OS maps 1:25000 133 Haslemere, 1:50000 186 Aldershot.

Start from the layby beside the B3004 in East Worldham, SU 749 380, or from the village green at Oakhanger, SU 770 362. Hartley Mauditt has parking spots.

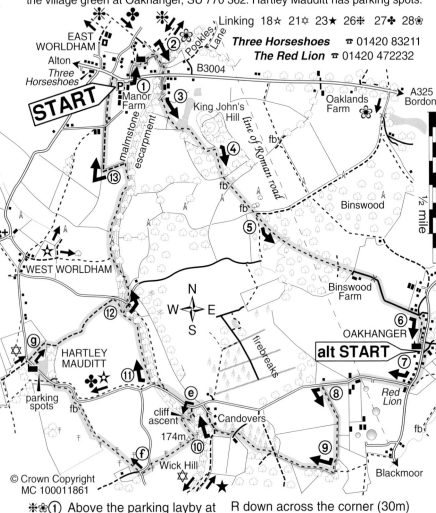

Linking 18★ 21✿ 23★ 26❋ 27♣ 28❀

Three Horseshoes ☎ 01420 83211
The Red Lion ☎ 01420 472232

❋❀① Above the parking layby at East Worldham, follow the lane L to the church (100m). Enter the churchyard via the drive R, pass R of the church and out along the (rat trap) wall to the large field (150m).
② Go R down the edge of the field and through the gate (100m). Bear R down across the corner (30m) and exit past Old School House to the road (30m). Cross slightly R and take the R farm track (150m).
③ From the R bend, bear L down through the large field, past the protruding corner of the vineyard, to the far end of the ponds (200m).

76

Cross the dam (50m) and follow the line of trees across the foot of King John's Hill to the gate (150m). In the wood keep on to the corner of the field (100m).

④ Turn R down through the wood to the next field (200m). Go straight over to the corner (70m). Stay on the same line across the next field, centrally between the pylons to the Binswood gate (200m).

⑤ A path goes L along the edge and two public footpaths go into the wood. Take the L pf, a faint path across the wood (SE) to Binswood Farm (800m). Carry on ahead on the track past the farm buildings and between the fields (600m).

⑥ When the track bends L near houses at Oakhanger, take the path R behind gardens and join the road at the village green near the church (150m). ★ Go on (R) along the road to the **Red Lion** (300m).

⑦ Go up the side road R, past the radomes L, round L & R bends at the farm (450m) and on (200m).

⑧ Opposite the pumping station R disregard the gate to the field L but enter the next field at stile or gate. Follow the L edge along the fields to the corner with trees (550m).

⑨ Go round the corner R and up the L edge to the wood (400m). Keep to the uphill track ahead through the wood (300m). Cross the track from the field L and curve L on the path into the field (40m). Go up the R edge, right into the corner (150m). ☿

⑩ Join the track at the foot of the malmscarp and turn R. Pass the houses of Candovers and follow the drive to the road (150m). Walk up the road L (100m). ♣☆

ⓔ *Extension up dangerous cliff to Hartley Mauditt: Turn L on the track into the trees (30m). Bear R up the side path and climb the malmscarp (40m). In the field go along the L edge to the power lines (200m) and R with the cables over the field past the trig point to the trees (400m) then L to the road (100m).*

ⓕ *Cross the road R up into the field. Aim slightly L past the corner of the garden to the electricity pole before the hedge and continue in the same line to the hedge (400m). Cross the culvert and follow the hedge R to the road (400m). Go on (L) along the road (300m).*

ⓖ *Soon after the pond turn R on the farm track which wanders over the fields (800m). Ultimately pass round the corner above the hanger to the side path L (100m). ➧⑫*

⑪ Keep on up the road (200m). Don't join the path beside the field but just after it take the path above the road R up the hanger (70m). Turn R along the edge of the field at the top of the hanger (550m) to the path R, 100m before the corner.

⑫ Drop down the stepped path (30m). Cross the road and follow the track opposite to the field (150m). Just along the top edge (60m) take the path L obliquely up the malmscarp (100m) and carry on along the R edge of the field (150m), and the next (550m).

⑬ At the next corner go L up the end of the field (200m) then R on the track towards Manor Farm (300m). Cross the drive, pass L of the house into the field and go on along the edge to the road in East Worldham (300m) below the layby (**Three Horseshoes** 150m L).

39 Kingsley Mill and Wyck

About 8½ km/5¼ miles with a short cut of 2 km/1¼ miles; farmland and woods; long views and short bone-shaker descents on the malmscarp; lots of stiles; not much shade. OS maps 1:25000 144 Basingstoke, 1:50000 186 Aldershot.

Start at the car park near Kingsley pond, SU 788 381.

Linking walks   28✹   34★   40☆

The Cricketers ☎ 01420 476730

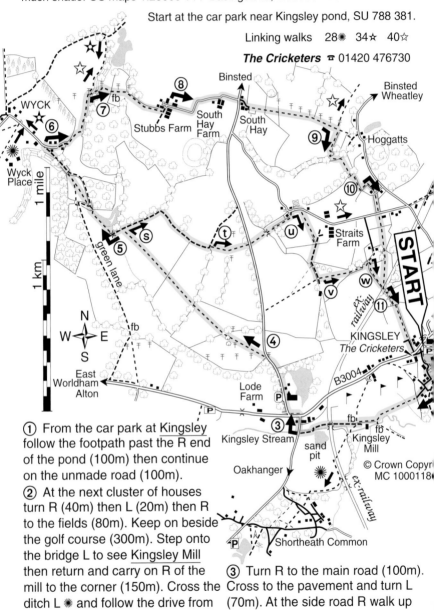

① From the car park at Kingsley follow the footpath past the R end of the pond (100m) then continue on the unmade road (100m).

② At the next cluster of houses turn R (40m) then L (20m) then R to the fields (80m). Keep on beside the golf course (300m). Step onto the bridge L to see Kingsley Mill then return and carry on R of the mill to the corner (150m). Cross the ditch L ✹ and follow the drive from the mill over the Bordon Railway embankment and the Kingsley Stream to the road (400m).

③ Turn R to the main road (100m). Cross to the pavement and turn L (70m). At the side road R walk up past the old church (100m). Keep on past the house to the first field L after the L curve (300m).

④ At the start of the R curve, enter the field L. Cross ½R to a gateway just after the power cables halfway along the hedge (350m). In the next field aim 40m L of the far R corner (250m). In the next field go straight on (250m) towards distant houses. Keep to the same line in the next field. Aim 50m R of the L end of the trees at the far edge (450m). Join the track.

Ⓢ *Short cut of 2 km/1¼ miles: Follow the track up R, round the R bend (300m) to the L bend (450m).*

Ⓣ *Just round the bend cross the fields R directly to the tree-lined road (250m). Stay ahead opposite down to the stream (200m) and up beside the hedge past the house L then cross the end of the garden L up to the road (150m). ☆*

Ⓤ *Walk along the road R (80m). On the bend take the footpath R down between fields (250m). At the bottom join the track from Straits Farm and follow it across the field R (150m) then along the L edge of the next field (150m).*

Ⓥ *Before the shed, on the cross path from the hedge, turn L over the field to the far corner (200m). Go on through the belt of trees to the corner of the R field (120m).*

Ⓦ *Enter the little field ahead and turn R into the adjacent field (10m). Follow the R edge to the next corner (200m). ➔⑪*

⑤ Go L (50m), over the stream and R up the edge of the field past the pond (250m). At the trees turn R (20m) then L into the trees to the next field (20m). Go straight up to the top L corner (300m). Continue on the track up the malmscarp to the road in Wyck (200m). ☆

⑥ Turn back R to the end of the tarmac and keep on into the field (150m). Go L along the hedge (80m). When it bends L stay ahead crossing obliquely to the R edge (100m) then beside the trees on the edge of the malmscarp watching out for the path down R (350m). ☆

⑦ Drop down through the hanger and cross the footbridge at the bottom of the valley (150m). Go straight up to the protruding hedge corner (120m) and continue up the L hedge to the farm (300m).

⑧ At the large barns turn L to the farmyard and follow the lane R over the rise to the road in the valley at South Hay (600m). Go up the track opposite (200m), straight over the fields, past a hedge end L on top (350m) and down to a path junction on the brow of the hill (200m).☆

⑨ Turn R. Avoid the path into the adjacent field and follow the L edge to the bottom corner (200m). Drop through the trees (60m) and cross the next field to the stile (100m). Drop through the next trees (40m) to another field and follow the L edge down to the corner (100m).

⑩ Go L (50m) & R (60m) outside the garden. Cross the drive and go down the path opposite between fields (100m). Over the road stay ahead between fields (250m). Keep on past the fence corner R (50m) then aim slightly R for the furthest corner of the field (200m).

⑪ Cross the embankment of the ex-Bordon Railway (20m) and follow the R hedge (100m). Just round the corner, pass into the next field and follow the L edge then the track to Kingsley (350m). The car park is 50m L from the ***Cricketers***.

A325 Bordon

40 Kingsley, Binsted and Wheatley

About 10 km/6½ miles or two 6 km/4 mile walks, heath and farmland; several short steep slopes. OS maps 1:25000 144 Basingstoke, 1:50000 186 Aldershot.

Start from the heath car park at the pond near Kingsley Church, SU 788 381. Alternatively start from Binsted, parking beside the village street or at the recreation ground, SU 773 410 (entrance drive opposite the pub).

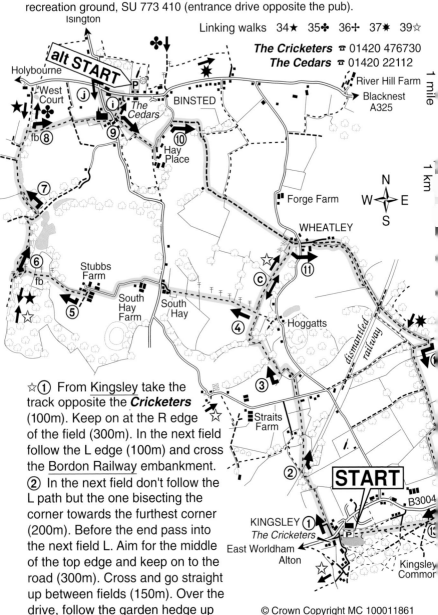

Linking walks 34★ 35♣ 36✛ 37✷ 39☆

The Cricketers ☎ 01420 476730
The Cedars ☎ 01420 22112

☆① From Kingsley take the track opposite the **Cricketers** (100m). Keep on at the R edge of the field (300m). In the next field follow the L edge (100m) and cross the Bordon Railway embankment.
② In the next field don't follow the L path but the one bisecting the corner towards the furthest corner (200m). Before the end pass into the next field L. Aim for the middle of the top edge and keep on to the road (300m). Cross and go straight up between fields (150m). Over the drive, follow the garden hedge up then L into the field (120m).

© Crown Copyright MC 100011861

③ Go up the R edge (100m), L round the corner (20m) then up the steep malmscarp under the trees, straight up the next field (100m) and more malmscarp (30m). In the next field follow the R edge (200m).

ⓒ *Short cut: Ahead (550m).* ➔⑪

④ At the 4-path junction turn up the field past a hedge end (200m). Go straight on over the fields and down the track to the road at South Hay (700m). Keep on up the lane opposite winding past barns on top and down to Stubbs Farm (600m).

⑤ After barns and just before the farmhouse turn L to the field and R down the edge. When the hedge bends R (300m) cross slightly L to the bottom of the valley (120m). Over the footbridge go straight up into the trees. Slightly L climb the stepped malmscarp path (100m). ★

⑥ Turn R on the path along the top edge of the hanger (400m).

⑦ Round the end of the field, drop down the stepped path. Turn R on the track (50m) then L on the side path up the R edge of the field with ponds (500m). After the track L with a hedge, watch out for the stepped side path R in the trees (100m). ❧

⑧ Cross the little valley up to the field and go straight over to the hedge (300m). Follow the hedge R & L to Binsted Church (100m). See Monty's grave at the start of the churchyard and go on, R of the church, to the road (200m). ✳

ⓘ *If visiting the **Cedars** continue ahead on the path opposite between little fields and houses to the road (100m) then R (100m).*

ⓙ *If starting at Binsted go down the street from the pub (200m) then L to the church (200m).*

⑨ Join the path opposite the main gate of the churchyard. Don't go straight on but take the side path R beside the village hall and straight over the fields (400m). At the road go L past Hay Place and on (200m).

⑩ After the modern house turn R down the track and stay on it all the way to the end. It bends R (250m) down over a malmstone ravine, then follows the L edge of the fields, bending L near a malmstone barn (350m) and again at the houses at Wheatley (750m).

ⓒ *Short cut: Turn R on the path across the field (550m).* ➔④

⑪ Cross the road and carry on (70m). After the (converted) hop kilns, enter the R field and follow the edge (600m) then re-join the bridleway L. Stay ahead between the fields, over a track (ex Bordon Railway) into the long narrow field (150m) and along the edge of the wood to the end of the field (400m).

⑫ Enter the field ahead and go R round the hedge bend to the corner (150m). Go L round the corner and on along the R edge from field to field past a track R (300m) to a rounded corner (250m). Enter the field with the pond ahead and go round the R corner. Keep on at R edges to the road (450m). Cross into Kingsley Common and go down the track a bit (60m).

⑬ Near the fork turn R on the side path (70m) then R along the track, round L and on (150m). Just after the ½L branch track (20m) diverge R along the side path (450m). At the pond transfer to the path on the bank but keep on in the same direction to the car park near Kingsley Church (100m).

41 Alice Holt and River Hill

About 9 km/5½ miles, mainly in oak and conifer woods. The 2¾ km/1¾ mile extension is boggy in winter. OS 1:25000 144+145, 1:50000 186 Aldershot.

Start from Bentley Station, SU 791 430, at weekends when parking is free or from the small forest car park off Gravel Hill Road near the route, SU 802 433. On the extension, start from the Abbotts Wood car park, SU 810 410.

Linking walks 33 ✿ 37 ✳ 12 ❋ 13 ✡ 14 ✦ 15 ✾

The Jolly Farmer ☎ 01420 22244

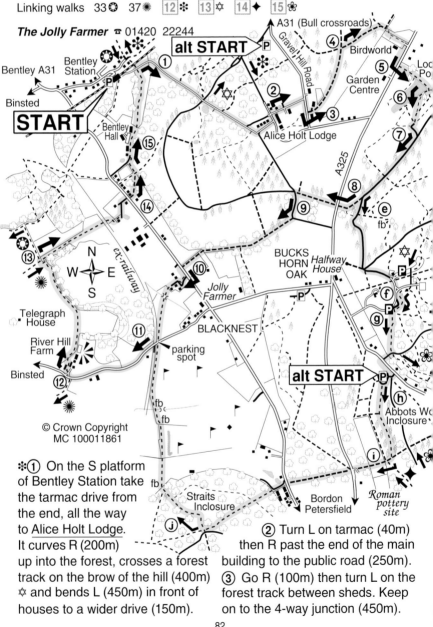

✳① On the S platform of Bentley Station take the tarmac drive from the end, all the way to Alice Holt Lodge. It curves R (200m) up into the forest, crosses a forest track on the brow of the hill (400m) ✡ and bends L (450m) in front of houses to a wider drive (150m).

② Turn L on tarmac (40m) then R past the end of the main building to the public road (250m).

③ Go R (100m) then turn L on the forest track between sheds. Keep on to the 4-way junction (450m).

④ Turn along the R track (300m). When it bends R to the boundary (50m), exit R along the L edge of the Birdworld car parks (200m).

⑤ Don't cross the road yet but go R until opposite the opening after the garden fences L (150m). Cross into the forest passing the L end of Lodge Pond (250m).

⑥ Turn R along the edge of the pond but soon diverge L on a side path up to the anglers' car park (250m) and follow the track to the major forest hard track (100m).

⑦ Go R to the fork where the main track bends L (500m).

ⓔ *Extension of 2¾ km/1¾ miles: Stay on the main track round into the dip, up, down, up L to tarmac (700m). Go past the main Forest Centre car park to the junction near the café cabin. Cross to the pond in the dip (100m).* ✦

ⓕ *Turn R on the path curving R beside the trees (200m).*

ⓖ *Several paths branch L. Take the last one (Easy Access) from the corner of the small car park to the cross track (250m). ❀ Turn R to the road (100m) then L (100m).*

ⓗ *Turn R to the Abbotts Wood car park. Follow the L edge to the clearing (100m) and keep on down the path to the end (550m).*

ⓘ *Turn R to the field (50m). Go straight over and out to the road (200m). Follow the main track ahead (450m), over another road and up beside the hedge into the corner (100m). Take the path ahead through forest to the cross path near the hard track L (500m).*

ⓙ *Go R on the cross path, round the L bend (150m) to the edge of the forest (350m) and ½R over the*

field to the trees at the hedge-corner (150m). Carry on at the L edge of the golf course all the way to the road (750m). Turn L. ✦⑪

⑧ Take the lesser track ahead (200m), over the road and on to the 4-way junction (300m).

⑨ Go L on the hard track (200m). On the L bend take the branch track R all the way to Blacknest (800m).

⑩ Turn L along the road (50m). At the track R to houses, enter the R garden and go L round the hedge to the next gate (100m). Outside, follow the track R to the end house. Go along the garden path and past the front door. Carry on over the fields behind, via the footbridge, to the top L corner (400m).

⑪ Walk up the road R (650m). ✳

⑫ At River Hill Farm climb the steep path L of the drive. Keep to the edge of the bank above the buildings to the field (100m) and R round the edge. When the edge bends R (150m) go straight over to the nearest trees (Telegraph House visible L) and carry on above the malmstone escarpment (500m). ❍

⑬ From the jutting corner go R down the next fields and over the Bordon Railway cutting (500m). Cross the next field obliquely R to the corner (50m) and carry on outside the field to the farm track (50m) then L to the road (150m).

⑭ Slightly R on the other side pass between the gardens then ½L through the trees (200m). At the field don't join the cross path but keep on (100m).

⑮ At the track go R to the end (200m) and on down the butterfly meadow to the forest drive (350m). Bentley Station is L (100m).

42 Priors Dean and Colemore

About 7½ km/4¾ miles with two extensions of 3 km/1¾ mile to Colemore and 4½ km/2¾ mile to Hawkley. A hilly walk on the chalk. Farmland and woods. Splendid views. OS maps 1:25000 133 Haslemere, 1:50000 186 Aldershot.

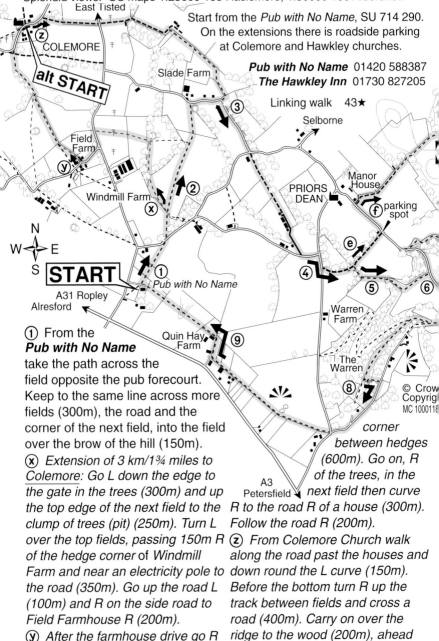

Start from the *Pub with No Name*, SU 714 290. On the extensions there is roadside parking at Colemore and Hawkley churches.

Pub with No Name 01420 588387
The Hawkley Inn 01730 827205

Linking walk 43★

① From the **Pub with No Name** take the path across the field opposite the pub forecourt. Keep to the same line across more fields (300m), the road and the corner of the next field, into the field over the brow of the hill (150m).

ⓧ *Extension of 3 km/1¾ miles to Colemore: Go L down the edge to the gate in the trees (300m) and up the top edge of the next field to the clump of trees (pit) (250m). Turn L over the top fields, passing 150m R of the hedge corner of Windmill Farm and near an electricity pole to the road (350m). Go up the road L (100m) and R on the side road to Field Farmhouse R (200m).*

ⓨ *After the farmhouse drive go R down the edge of the fields to the*

corner between hedges (600m). Go on, R of the trees, in the next field then curve R to the road R of a house (300m). Follow the road R (200m).

ⓩ *From Colemore Church walk along the road past the houses and down round the L curve (150m). Before the bottom turn R up the track between fields and cross a road (400m). Carry on over the ridge to the wood (200m), ahead down to the next field, along the R*

84

edge (250m) and round the L bend. Halfway to the R bend (30m), turn R on the path along the bottom of the fields past a farm far R (400m). Before the steep part diverge R to the top R corner (200m). Go out R (30m) and turn L on the road. →③

② Go down the field to pass round the clump of trees at the L edge near the bottom (500m) and on to the road opposite the farmhouse (200m). Turn R up the road past the houses (250m).

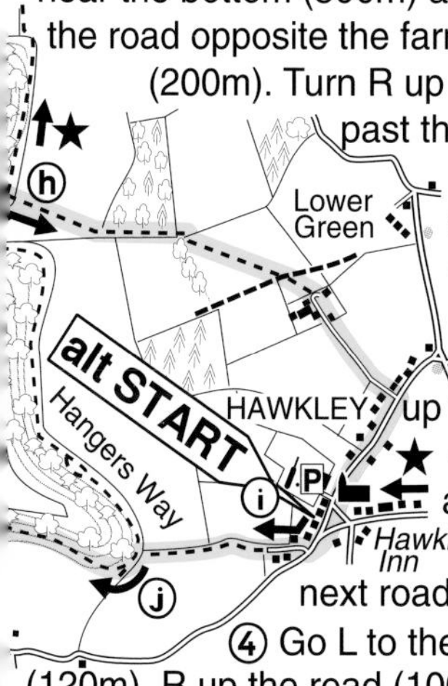

③ Keep on to the junction (400m), up the track opposite and down to the next road (500m).

④ Go L to the junction (120m), R up the road (100m) & L down the track under trees (200m).

Ⓔ *Extension of 4½ km/2¾ miles to Hawkley: Stay on the track to the bottom (300m). Go L on the road to the house at Priors Dean (250m).*

Ⓕ *Turn R along the garden wall. Go up the L edge of the field to the top corner (500m), out through the trees, up over the ridge R of the hedge, and down R of the wood to the L corner of the field (500m).*

Ⓖ *Turn into the trees and curve R down the hanger obliquely to the path junction at the Hangers Way outside a corner of field (300m).* ★

Ⓗ *Turn back L down the path (30m) then R into the field. Cross to the R corner of the wood opposite (250m). Go up the R edge (200m), over the R fields obliquely towards*

Map labels: Lower Green · alt START · Hangers Way · HAWKLEY · P · Hawkley Inn · ⓗ · ⓘ · ⓙ · ★

the R edge of the L house (300m), up the drive to Hawkley (300m). and R along the road (300m).

Ⓘ *From Hawkley Church walk to the furthest corner of the village green (100m) and on along the road. Round the bend (50m) turn R up the drive behind houses (100m). Continue at the R edge of the field (300m) and into the wood.*

Ⓙ *Carry on L round the end of the hill rising gently (500m). At the first field R stay in the trees (250m). At the next field, cross the corner into the trees again (80m) and continue on the winding path down to the road (300m). Turn back L down the steep road (300m).* →⑥

⑤ At the widening and slight twist in the track turn R up between the fields and into a field (100m). Go down the L edge (150m) then drop through the hanger to the field below (100m) and follow the L edge over to the road (200m). Turn R.

⑥ Stay on the road to the track R (Doscombe) at the pond (400m).

⑦ Go up the track (150m). After the house continue up the steep path (100m) and fork R up through Warren Nature Reserve (100m). After the L bend keep to the gently rising path on the steep valleyside to the stepped zigzag path L before the fence (500m).

⑧ Go up the zizag (100m) and carry on along the road (R) to the junction near houses at Warren Corner (500m). Opposite, carry on along the footpath in the fields to the corner at the farm (1000m).

⑨ Turn R along the edge (150m) then L (150m). Stay ahead in a straight line over the fields to the *Pub with No Name* (600m).

43 Hawkley, the Hangers Way and Noar Hill

About 9 km/5½ miles. The extension of 1½ km/1 mile and short cut of 400m/¼ mile may be used together. Farmland and woods; long steep climbs. Lots of stiles. OS maps 1:25000 133 Haslemere 1:50000 186 Aldershot.

Start from Hawkley village hall car park or beside the village green, SU 745 291.

Linking walks   24✳   42★   44❄

The Hawkley Inn ☎ 01730 827205

① From Hawkley Church walk to the furthest corner of the village green (100m) and on along the road (50m). Just round the bend turn R up the drive behind the houses (100m). At the end carry on down the R edge of the field and up into the <u>hanger</u> (300m).

ⓔ *Extension of 1½ km/1 mile to Priors Dean: Go L round the end of the hill, rising gently (500m). At the* first field R stay in the trees (250m). *At the next field, cross the corner into the trees (80m) and keep on down (250m) ★ Go on (R) along the road to the 1st house R (450m).*

ⓕ *Turn R along the garden wall and go up the L edge of the field to the top corner (500m), out through the trees, up over the ridge R of the hedge, and down R of the wood to the L corner of the field (500m).*

ⓖ *Turn into the trees and curve R down the hanger obliquely to the path junction at the Hangers Way outside a field (300m). Turn L.* ➜③

② Go R on the path along the foot of the hanger, the Hangers Way, (750m), L & R round a field to the path junction (250m) then down R.

③ Keep to the foot of the hanger, disregarding paths to the fields R (400m). When the hanger bends L carry on ahead outside the L field and over the footbridge in the defile (150m). Cross the next field ahead to the far R corner (250m).

④ Go out R along the end of the next field (200m). On the road walk L past the houses, over the rise and down (200m). ✳

⑤ Just before the house near the bottom turn R into the field. Follow the L edge (200m) and go straight over the next field in the same line to the far L corner then out to the road L (250m). Cross slightly R to the field opposite. Follow the path at the R edge (50m) then cross to the adjacent field and diverge from the fence up to the stile at the hanger. In the trees the path bends ½L. Keep on up to the brow of Noar Hill (300m). ✳

⑥ Turn R on the path along the brow, soon beside a field (450m). Fork R from the Hangers Way and gently descend (450m). Avoid the diverging path L near the foot and continue down into the field (70m).

⑦ Turn back R along the top edge of the fields to the end of the 2nd field (500m) then follow the fence down (100m). Cross the next field towards the far R corner (100m). L of it, pass between gardens to the road at Empshott Green (70m).

⑧ Carry on over the field opposite (200m). Outside, follow the track L down to the road (350m). Turn R down the road (70m) then L on the path into the trees (but go on 80m to Hawkley Mill first). Cross the infant River Rother and ascend briefly (100m). Turn L along the foot of the escarpment and keep on to the next large field (500m). ❇

ⓢ *Short cut of 400m/¼ mile: Go up the R edge (100m). Stay ahead up the track to the houses (600m) and up the drive to the steep side path L at the R bend (100m).*

ⓣ *Climb to the corner of the field and follow the L edge to the road (350m). Go L on the road past the farm to the next track R (200m).* ➜⑪

⑨ Go straight down, over the stream into the next field (100m) then make for the trees at the top L corner. The right of way is up the R edge (250m) and across above the shed (150m) but there is usually a more direct oblique path (450m).

⑩ Cross into the next field and turn R up the edge. Continue up into the wood to join another path on a bend (150m). Keep on (L) into the next field (50m). Follow the undulating R edge (350m). Just into the next field turn R up through the hanger to the fields on top (150m). Keep to the L edge from field to field. When the edge curves slightly L (200m) stay ahead towards a barn beyond the road (200m). Turn R on the road to the next track on the other side (70m).

⑪ Turn into the track to the barn. Keep on at the R edge of the field to the road junction (350m) and on the road ahead to the **Hawkley Inn** (250m) and village green (100m).

44 Greatham, Empshott (and Temple Manor)

About 7 km/4½ miles over undulating farmland and orchards; with an extension of 4 km/2½ miles to Temple Manor; short steep climbs through the hangers; lots of stiles. OS maps 1:25000 133 Haslemere, 1:50000 186 Aldershot.

Start at Greatham; park in the layby south of the church, SU 773 303.

Linking walk 43❋

The Greatham Inn 01420 538016

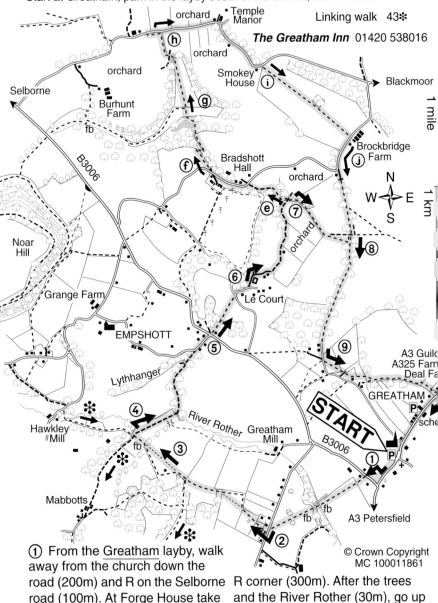

① From the Greatham layby, walk away from the church down the road (200m) and R on the Selborne road (100m). At Forge House take the path L to the field (100m). Go straight over to the trees near the R corner (300m). After the trees and the River Rother (30m), go up the next field to the stile 150m R of the top L corner (300m).

② Just along the road L (60m) take the footpath R at the first drive. Skirt the garden R (20m), cross the hedge and go L to the fields (30m). Go up the fields from stile to stile at far R corners (400m). On top follow the line of trees ahead to the next field (200m) and go on to the corner of the wood (50m). ❇

③ The public footpath is across above the shed and down the far edge but there is usually a direct path to the bottom L corner (450m). Cross the footbridge and go up towards the gate (80m). ❇

④ Before the gate turn R on the track down the middle of the long field to the gate at the bottom end (350m). Go on up the winding track to the lane at Empshott (450m) and down R to the main road (150m).

⑤ Follow the footpath opposite up through the wood (150m) then up the field to the high point (150m). Walk along the drive ahead (100m).

⑥ On a slight bend take the side track L up around the Le Court site and down round a R bend past the end houses to the orchard (100m). Go through, keeping to the main track L of a building, skirting the foot of the steep slope, then beside trees, up to the gateway (500m).

> The orchards belong to the Blackmoor Estate. Planting started in 1946 on the malmstone fields above the frost traps and there are now 250 acres of plums, apples and pears. Fruit is sold at the estate yard near Blackmoor Church.

ⓔ *Extension of 4 km/2½ miles to Temple Manor: Outside the gate take the path L up into the hanger then R round the edge of the trees to the field gate. Go out on the track to the lane at Bradshott Hall (300m) and up the lane L (250m).*

ⓕ *Turn R at the first field on top. Go round the R edge (200m) then zigzag down to the field below and keep on into the corner (150m). Walk down through the trees past the end of the pond (60m) then L to the fields (100m).*

ⓖ *Go straight up the fields into the arms of the hanger. Exit L of the apex and climb to the orchard (400m). Turn R, not on the farm track, but on the other side of the wind-break hedge and carry on beside it to join the lane (100m).*

ⓗ *Go R on the lane, round the bend at Temple Manor (450m) and down to the L bend (500m).*

ⓘ *From the side track, just round the bend (30m), go straight down the middle of the field aiming for the farm at the far end. Exit at the gate opposite the R barn (750m).*

ⓙ *Follow the lane R to the bend (250m). Fork L on the track before the house and carry on ahead through the trees (400m). ➔⑧*

⑦ Go R down the path outside the orchard fence (150m). After the wood stay at the R edge of the field until it bends R (200m) then drop L straight down the track to the belt of trees below (200m) and join the path a little way in (20m). Turn R

⑧ Stay on the path all the way to the houses (800m) and ahead on the lane to the drive R (100m).

⑨ Just after it (20m), enter the field L. Diverge from the lane to the furthest corner (150m) and go on between fields and gardens (150m). At the large field follow the R edge all the way to Deal Farm. Pass R of the garden to the road (500m).

⑩ Cross to the pavement and walk R to the layby (500m).

45 Winchester and St Catherine's Hill

About 6¾ km/4½ miles via the city centre, water meadows and St Cross with an extension of 3½ km/2¼ miles over Twyford Down. OS maps 1:25000 132 Winchester, 1:50000 185 Winchester.

Start from Garnier Road car park, SU 483 280.

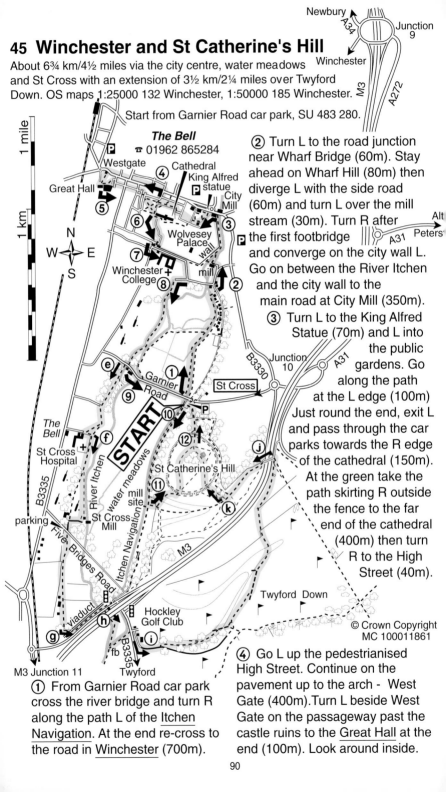

The Bell
☎ 01962 865284

② Turn L to the road junction near Wharf Bridge (60m). Stay ahead on Wharf Hill (80m) then diverge L with the side road (60m) and turn L over the mill stream (30m). Turn R after the first footbridge and converge on the city wall L. Go on between the River Itchen and the city wall to the main road at City Mill (350m).

③ Turn L to the King Alfred Statue (70m) and L into the public gardens. Go along the path at the L edge (100m) Just round the end, exit L and pass through the car parks towards the R edge of the cathedral (150m). At the green take the path skirting R outside the fence to the far end of the cathedral (400m) then turn R to the High Street (40m).

④ Go L up the pedestrianised High Street. Continue on the pavement up to the arch - West Gate (400m). Turn L beside West Gate on the passageway past the castle ruins to the Great Hall at the end (100m). Look around inside.

① From Garnier Road car park cross the river bridge and turn R along the path L of the Itchen Navigation. At the end re-cross to the road in Winchester (700m).

90

⑤ Go down the broad steps past the County Court. Bear L down more steps and over the courtyard to the road (120m). Turn R away from the main road (30m) then L down St Clement Street, over two crossroads to the bottom (200m). Slightly R (20m) take the passage to the next road (25m) and cross obliquely to the cathedral (150m).

⑥ Go through the passage way R of the cathedral then follow the drive across the close winding L then R to the close studded and jettied Cheney Court (250m). Turn R through Priory Gate and L under St Swithun's Church (50m).

⑦ Go L along College Street past Jane Austen's Lodgings R and Winchester College R to Wolvesey Palace L (250m). Turn R with the road (100m) and R along College Walk behind the college (120m).

⑧ Turn L on the footpath beside the stream. Keep on between the winding River Itchen L and sports fields R to Garnier Road (700m).

ⓔ *Extension of 3½ km/2¼ miles: Cross and continue on the path R of the stream past a road-end R (300m). After it (100m) diverge R to the next road (100m). (**The Bell** is 200m along the road.) Enter the gateway to see St Cross Hospital.*

ⓕ *Return to the meadow path and carry on (250m). In wet seasons stay ahead to the road (400m) but when dry, diverge L along the river bank to Saint Cross Mill (300m) then follow the drive R & L to the road (200m). Cross and carry on at the R edge of the fields (700m).*

ⓖ *Pass under the viaduct near the R end and turn L along the path beside the road (350m)*

ⓗ *Over the river, cross the road and take the path beside (L of) the river (250m). Turn L on the first side path and cross the road into Hockley golf club (200m).*

ⓘ *Go up the tarmac drive R and round the L curve (100m). Carry on up the track (200m). Just before the wood, transfer to the footpath L and go on through the trees above the fairway in the dry valley (400m). Eventually join a golf track obliquely up to a path junction at the brow on Twyford Down (50m). Turn L along the brow and continue on the golf track (500m). Curve L across the fairway near the top of the valley and go up the path L of the cleft (old path) and ahead past a golfers' footbridge from the cleft into the level field (150m). Cross to the M3 cutting (180m) and bear R along the edge past the Ravage memorial to the bridge (300m).*

ⓙ *Cross and go down the main valley path to the first side path R after the trees (450m).*

ⓚ Follow paths straight up (150m), over the Iron Age ramparts and R of the summit trees (300m). ➤⑫

⑨ Turn L to the car park (500m).

⑩ Go through the car park and on along the footpath beside the Navigation past the hill L (750m).

⑪ Turn L up the side path in the dry valley (50m) and turn up the stepped path L to the Iron Age ramparts (200m). Follow the path L of the summit trees (300m).

⑫ On the brow of St Catherine's Hill overlooking Winchester, identify the cathedral and aim down toward it. Join the main path through the ramparts and keep on always downwards to the car park (350m).

Alice Holt Forest is on land the Forestry Commission acquired in 1924. Most of it is plantations for logging and research but open to riders and walkers. The underlying Gault clay is too heavy for normal agriculture but sustains oak. Patches of Ice Age gravel overlying the clay are planted with conifers.

Holt was a Saxon word for wood. *Alice* may derive from the Saxon personal name, Ælfsige, diminutive Alfsi, possibly the Bishop of Winchester from 951. The Saxon hunting area which included Woolmer Forest, largely owned by the Bishops of Winchester, became one of the first designated forests under the Normans. The first keeper was probably Geoffrey the Marshall, Lord of the Domesday Book manor of Worldham, whose de Venuz descendants were hereditary keepers. A record survives of a perambulation of the forest in 1171. The hammer beam roof of the Palace of Westminster was prefabricated at Farnham using Alice Holt oaks when it was re-roofed for Richard II in 1394. A survey in 1608 declared 13,031 trees suitable for the Royal Navy.

Alice Holt Lodge is now a research station of the Forestry Commission with laboratories, library and trial plots, complementing the work of the northern station near Edinburgh. The research and advisory service covers propagation, pathology and breeding of trees, pest control, ecology and recreation. The house was built around 1816. It was used as a military hospital in World War I. The Forestry Commission bought it in 1946. The medieval Great Lodge for the Ranger or Lieutenant of the Forest may have been here, though Gilbert White thought it was on the site of Jenkyn Place in Bentley. Sir William Sandys wrote of living in the Great Lodge in 1530 when he was Henry VIII's Ranger. Ruperta Howe, daughter of Prince Rupert and actress Peg Hughes, was Ranger from 1709. Her husband released boar and buffalo which the locals promptly killed.

Alton was two manors at AVLTONE in the Domesday Book, one retained by the king and the other given to the Abbot at Winchester in exchange for a house there. The present town has spread over land of two other manors HANSIGE, Anstey, and WILDEHEL, Will Hall. Alton became a market town by acquiring the market of Neatham and may thus be the heir to the Roman town there. Its enterprises related to the countryside - cloth, hops and brewing, with the Wey to power mills and a good position on the road from Winchester and the coast to London. The main church, St Lawrence, dates from about 1080. The Cavaliers lost the Battle of Alton but impeded the Roundheads' advance on Winchester. Fanny Adams lies in the town cemetery. She was an 8-year old from Tanhouse Lane, murdered in 1867, butchered and scattered around the hop fields. The outcry in the newspapers coincided with the novelty of canned food in the Royal Navy and *Sweet FA* is said to derive from matelots' macabre mutterings on the contents of pusser tins. The murderer, Frederick Baker, was the last person hanged in public at Winchester.

The **Alton-Farnham** railway line was an extension of the LSWR (London & SW Railway Co) which opened in 1852. At that time the London trains arrived via Guildford and Tongham but they now travel via Woking and Ash Vale.

Jane **Austen's House** is a museum, open daily for much of the year but only at weekends in winter. It is a private trust set up in 1949 by Thomas Carpenter as a memorial for his son killed in action in 1944.

The **Basingstoke-Alton** railway was 13 miles long with stations for Herriard, Bentworth & Lasham and Cliddesdon. It was opened 1901, taken up in WWI to supply track for France, restored in 1924 and closed in 1936. It appears to have been the first light railway, having received assent in January 1897, only five months after the Light Railways Act. It featured in the 1937 Will Hay film *Oh! Mr Porter*.　　　　*The Basingstoke and Alton Light Railway* M Dean et al 1998 128pp

Bentley was a Hampshire berewick of the great Surrey manor of Farnham in ancient times, given to the Abbey of Winchester by charter of King Cedwalla in 688, one of the earliest Anglo-Saxon documents. BENEDLEI is listed twice in the Domesday Book: the 10 hides held directly by the bishop and a small manor of William (the Archer). There was a mill taxed at 10s but no church. When the by-pass was built in 1994, the work exposed bronze age and Saxon habitation. The road through the village used to be the A31 on the line of the Pilgrim's Way from Winchester to Canterbury, sharing its ancient traffic with the Harow Way which delimits the parish along the ridge top to the north. The Open Book was designed by Lord Baden Powell who lived at Pax Hill.

Bentley Church, St Mary the Virgin, dates from around 1170. Features of interest: Norman north pillar, chapel and tower of about 1180; south chapel of about 1240, 12th century font bowl in Purbeck marble, 19th century table tombs and remarkable yews. It did not have a rector until 1864. The tithes were allocated to Waverley Abbey which supplied preachers. After the Dissolution of the Monasteries the tithes went to the Archdeacon of Surrey who kept up the tradition with a perpetual curacy. Jane Austen's brother, Henry, was the curate in 1816 and lived at The Old Parsonage.

Bentworth does not appear in the Domesday Book but is probably included in the tax assessment of the large royal manor of Odiham. Henry I made it into an estate for Geoffrey, Archbishop of Rouen. Documents survive for this transfer around 1112. Archbishop Odon Rigaud is known to have visited in 1248. The Archbishop of York annexed it when estates were taken from alien houses during the Hundred Years' War. The manor house for many centuries was La Aule, the Hall, now Hall Farmhouse. Bentworth Lodge is Victorian.

Bentworth Church, St Mary, is 12th century, much restored in the Victorian era. The flint surface and Bath stone date from 1890. Points of interest: 12th century lancet chancel windows; Norman pillars with scalloped capitals and transitional pointed arches; 13th century piscina; memorial to Nicholas Holdip 1590-1606 SE in the chancel; arms of George IV; list of rectors from 1298.

Bentworth - the making of a Hampshire village Georgia Smith 1988 61pp

Binsted was BENESTEDE in the Domesday Book. After the Conquest it became part of the lands of Bishop Odo of Bayeux, William the Conqueror's half brother, but like all of his land in Hampshire was farmed to Hugh de Port. With "land for one plough" it would have been an island in the great royal manor of Neatham. Nicholas Wadham (d. 1609), founder of the college, was a Lord of the Manor. The church, Holy Cross, built of malmstone, was founded about 1140 and had its aisles and tower added before 1200. Points of interest: Norman round arches in the chancel but flat pointed arches in the nave; the original lancet chancel windows; the mid-14th century marble effigy of Richard de Westcote in Crusader chain mail; the graves of Monty and the Bonham-Carters of Wyck Place at the west end of the churchyard.

Binswood is a surviving fragment of the ancient royal forest of Woolmer on the soggy Gault clay. It is a rare example of ancient pasture wood where cattle graze in an environment comparable with the habitat of their wild ancestors. It is an SSSI and belongs to the Woodland Trust which invites visitors to roam. The commoners still have rights of grazing, estovers (taking wood for fuel or construction) and turbary (turf for fuel or construction).

The **Bordon Railway** line opened from Bentley in 1905 and closed in 1966. It was built to carry soldiers returning from the Boer War but the army extended it to Longmoor then to Liss then to the Portsmouth main line. The Royal Engineers had 60 miles of track branching from it for railway training.

Bradley first comes to light in 909 in a charter of Edward the Elder confirming the Bishop of Winchester's holding of 5 hides. Domesday Book BRADELEI was leased from the bishop's great manor of Overton. The manor house was demolished by guns in 1630 to evict the owner for debt. The church, All Saints, was rebuilt in 1877 but parts of the chancel date from the early 13th century.

Burkham appears in a French document as a berewick (outlier) of the Bentworth estate given to the Archbishop of Rouen around 1112, hence the name. It was purchased from the manor of Bentworth in 1590 for £160. Home Farm is being planted by the Woodland Trust and is open to walkers.

The **butterfly meadow** at Bentley Station was acquired in1992 by Butterfly Conservation. It is part of an SSSI with a butterfly fauna of 30 species. The 9 acres are managed to promote a wide variety of meadow flowers in glades.

Candovers is a pleasant cluster of houses around the 18th century estate yard of Hartley Mauditt. It was owned by John de Candevere in 1290 and leased to Selborne Priory. It was called manor when it changed hands in 1562.

Chawton is CELTONE in the Domesday Book, one of the numerous Norman manors given to Hugh de Port whose family held it for 500 years. It was bought by Nicholas Knight in 1578 from whom it descended through various sons and cousins who changed their surnames to Knight, eventually to one who was Jane Austen's brother. The house, at the top of the drive past the church, is late 16th century in origin. The village street was the main London road to Gosport, but is now by-passed by the A32. The present church, St Nicholas, was rebuilt of flint and Bath stone in the 1870s by Sir Arthur Blomfield. Jane Austen's mother and sister are buried in the churchyard. The school opened in 1840. A church is first recorded in a 1291 tax assessment @ £8 13s 4d.

Chawton Park occupied hilltops capped with thick clay which was used for brickmaking and now sustains forestry plantation. The park pale is still very obvious over most of its length in Park, Ackender and Bushy Leaz Woods.

Cheney Court, a 15th century, jettied and close studded building, was the bishop's court. The Bishop was temporal Lord of the Manor to a large part of Winchester (Bishop's Soke) and held courts like any other great landowner.

Coldrey farm house has a fine Georgian façade but the rear is timber-framed and probably 15th century. This was the grange of Waverley Abbey. In the 1950s an archæologist found many Roman buildings in the fields around the house with 1st-4th century pottery but there has been no full excavation. Just over the old A31 was a Roman cemetery with 12 cremation urns.

Colemore is COLMERE in the Domesday Book, a 1 hide manor of Humphrey the Chamberlain which appears to correspond to Colemore Farm. Edward Knight, Jane Austen's brother owned it in 1815. A separate manor of Colemore was given to the Southwick Priory in 1198, confirmed in a charter by Richard I. The church, manor house and farm are a nucleus without a village but there is a scattering of houses in the rolling, wooded farmland. The redundant church, St Peter ad Vincula, was founded in the 12th century or earlier. The little windows of the north transept (S transept demolished) and the Purbeck marble font appear to be of this period. The advowson was being contested in 1221.

The **Convent** of St Lucy at Medstead runs a playgroup, a home for old ladies and a church for local Catholics. It opened in 1955 in the former Medstead Manor, whose facade dates from 1901. Lucy Filippini (1672-1732) was a pious but gifted and energetic orphan from Tuscany. She was called to Rome to involve herself in teacher training which resulted in the founding of a teaching order of nuns. They are now world-wide. Lucy was canonised in 1930.

Empshott has a church but no compact village. The old manor house was at Grange Farm, near the church, and is reputed to have been a hiding place for Charles II. In the Domesday Book it was HIBESETE, a small manor rated @ 1¼ hides, owned by Geoffrey the Marshall who also held East Worldham.

Farringdon had one r until the end of the 19th century. The Domesday Book FERENDONE belonged to Bosham church with Bishop Osbern of Exeter as Lord of the Manor, a Saxon endowment to finance the College at that church. Henry II sold off part, Faringdon Popham (village and land), leaving the rump for the church. Manor Farm was the manor house of Faringdon Episcopi. A letter to Arthur Lisle, Henry VIII's Lieutenant in Calais dated 11/10/1533 says:
there is no Comen Syknes within five miles of me, save only at Faringdon...
The church, All Saints has unequal Norman arches in the nave; transitional windows of 1370 beside the door, in ornate Decorated style with mullions to the top as in Perpendicular style; an austere Georgian pulpit. Gilbert White was a curate here; Selborne is the adjoining parish. The weird building, Massey's Folly, is used as the village hall. It was built with his own hands by the Rector of 1857-1919, the Rev T H Massey, for reasons unknown.

The **Forestry Commission** was set up in 1919 after World War I to organise the strategic supply of timber. It survives as a body providing policy, grants and advice but its commercial arm carries out planting and logging. It has an open access policy on its own land and maintains paths and bridleways.

Four Marks is said to get its name from stones marking the adjoining corners of four parishes: Medstead, Ropley, Chawton and Farringdon. The village is largely 20th century ribbon development along several roads and tracks. The church, the Good Shepherd, dates from 1953 and was preceded only by the tin church of 1891. Telegraph Lane gets its name from the semaphore station on the signalling line to Plymouth, of which a room survives in Semaphore Farm.
Four Marks - its life and origins Betty Mills 1995 209pp

Froyle is FROLI in the Domesday Book. Upper and Lower Froyle are at about the same altitude but Upper Froyle has larger houses and the church. After the Dissolution the manor was bought by William Jephson whose family built the house, Froyle Place, next to the church in 1588 (altered in Jacobean and Victorian times). The last lord of the manor, Sir Hubert Miller (d.1941) had Italian statues of the saints fixed to 18 houses. The Georgian Froyle House, was built in 1816 by the Burninghams, Irish nobility, who bought part of the estate. The Queen Anne Manor House was not a manor house but probably Home Farm. The church, Assumption of the Blessed Virgin Mary, is transitional, Early English/Decorated of about 1310. The nave and tower were re-built in 1722. Points of interest: the original chancel roof; a fine reticulate east window with medieval armorial glass, the brass for John Ligh of Coldrey, next to the altar, dated 1574; numerous hatchments hanging in the nave.
The Village of Saints - a little history John Willcocks 1996 39pp

The **Froyle chalkpit** still operates from time to time, produces up to 10,000 tons a year. The chalk is loosened by harrowing the surface, crushed by driving over it and sieved. Granules are spread at about 2 ton per acre.

Froyle Mill on the River Wey and parish boundary is probably on the site of one of the two Domesday Book mills taxed with Froyle.

Fulling Mill Cottage was originally two mill cottages. This was probably the site of one of the 8½ Domesday Book mills of Neatham but a fulling mill is first documented in 1578. Of the mill itself only the footings survive. A fulling mill was a giant washing machine for de-oiling wool after weaving. In the adjacent field the cloths were suspended on tenter hooks to resist shrinking.

The **gas regulation** station near the A31 at Upper Froyle is for stepping down the pressure where a major pipe supplies local pipes, analogous with an electricity transformer. The step here is 7 bar to 2 bar (100 psi to 30 psi). The pressure in domestic pipes is around 10 mB above atmospheric pressure. The large capped pipes are for testing and inspection.

Gilbert White Museum was the naturalist's house but is also a museum for Captain Oates who perished in 1912 during Scott's return journey from the South Pole. The house is much as Gilbert White knew it but the large room at the north end was added by the owners (Pears of the soap) around 1900.

The **Great Hall** in Winchester was built in the 1220s as the main assembly space for the Royal castle. It was the venue for the Winchester parliaments and for state trials. The round table, reputed to be King Arthur's, is only 600 years old. Henry VIII showed it off to the Hapsburg, Charles V, perhaps to impress him with the antiquity of the realm. The castle, of which parts round about can now be visited, held the English treasury, a gaol for political prisoners and royal apartments. Henry III and Arthur, Henry VIII's elder brother, were born here. The castle was demolished after the Civil War but the Great Hall was retained for its usefulness.

Greatham, pronounced Gret'm, was GRETEHÃ in the Domesday Book, a 1 hide manor in William the Conqueror's demesne taken from the Saxon estate of Queen Edith. Le Court was the site of the medieval manor house. The present village stretches along one of the great roads from London to Portsmouth, recently by-passed. The church, St John the Baptist, was built in 1875 with a spire added in 1897 to mark Queen Victoria's Diamond Jubilee. A dilapidated medieval church is 150m away.

A **haggis path** is an uncomfortable sideways sloping path which gets its name from tracks made by the hornless ruminant indigenous to Scottish mountains. The animal is adapted for highland life by having shorter legs on the left side. Occasional mutants have short right legs causing them to feed in the opposite direction. Heterozygy appears to be promoted because mutants meet more individuals and have more opportunities to breed. Gillies developed the ingenious hunting technique of startling the animals in such a way that they turn round and thus fall over, hence the adjective haggard. Tales of animals with tartan colouration are feeble Sassenach (Saxon) humour.

Hanger is a Wealden word for a wood on a very steep slope. It may be specified as a yew or beech hanger etc. The Hangers Way is a 21 mile route along the chalk and malmstone hangers on the western lip of the Weald from Alton to south of Petersfield. The path was designated by Hants CC in 1990.

Hartley Mauditt is a deserted village. The houses were north of the church and the manor house was behind the church at the clump of trees. HERLEGE, the Domesday Book manor, was owned by William Mauduit. By inheritance and sale it passed through several noble owners including John of Gaunt. Lord Stawell, Chancellor of the Exchequer, pulled down the house around 1798, it is said, to stop his wife staying there when he had to live in London. The estate village withered, though there are still a few houses in the parish. The Church, St Leonard, is early 12th century. The horseshoe chancel arch and windows L of the pulpit and L of the door are early Norman. Points of interest: replaced doorway of around 1190, transitional with dogtooth pattern but pointed arch; 13th century chancel which probably replaced an apse; 14th century window near font and bell turret; a horseshoe and Lancaster rose in the tracery of the 15th century pulpit. The 14th century aumbrey and piscina appear low because the floor was raised in Victorian times.

Hawkley is a small village renowned as a centre for walking the hangers at the west end of the Weald. It is not in the Domesday Book probably being part of Newton Valence then. It is first recorded as the hamlet HAREKSLE in the grant of land to William de Valence in 1252 and there is mention of a chapel in 1291. It became a separate parish in 1860 and the present church, SS Peter & Paul is a spacious Gothic revival building of 1865 on the site of an earlier chapel of rest. Points of interest: the Rhenish Helm spire, carved capitals & corbels.

Hawkley Mill by the roadside is the millhouse - galetted malmstone. It bears a plaque inscribed: HOCHELEYE MILL seized from the Bishop of Winchester by Adam Gurdon. Given back 1280. Burnt 1771. Residence 1880.

Holybourne straddles the old London road from Alton and Gosport. Domesday Book records HALIBOURNE as a small manor in Neatham Hundred, owned in 1066 by Edward the Confessor but held by Wulfard. The church, Holy Rood, has a 12th century nave and tower and 13th century chancel. On the south side a buttress has a mass clock. The pond in the churchyard is fed by a spring and drains to the Wey via the Holy Bourne.

Isington Mill had two undershot wheels. Its 1899 sale price was £1800 with 4 pairs of stones. It was made into a house for Field Marshall Montgomery in 1947 and was his home until he died. Isington is a hamlet of Binsted.

The River **Itchen** is the brook in Cheriton which rises just south of the A272 and after only 20 miles is an arm of Southampton Water. It is known to have been navigable to Winchester in 1189 for in that year the bishop restored it; the Caen stone of the Cathedral pre-supposes water transport. The main work of the Navigation came after the Civil War and the first unladen boat arrived in 1697. It is only 10½ miles long and was never an economic success. It had 15 locks. The last boat to Winchester arrived in 1896.

King John's Hill, an outlier of malmstone on the Gault, was also known as Lodge Hill, being the site of a royal hunting lodge. The patent rolls show King John was here in 1204. The accounts for building or repairing the lodge survive: the cost was £88 4s 8d including 63,000 shingles and 3000 nails.

Kingsley is not listed in the Domesday Book. It was part of Woolmer Forest, an ancient Saxon hunting ground, and suddenly comes to light as a manor in 1466. The village lies in the valley of the Oxney Stream (River Slea) between the waterlogged clay of Alice Holt and the barren sands of Woolmer where the geological mix makes for fertile soil. There was a royal park here, hence the name, probably King's Meadow at Lode Farm which provided common grazing (Lammas land) for the tenants into the 20th century. Harry of Lode became Henry VIII. The church on the main road, All Saints, was built in 1876. An older church, St Nicholas, near Lode Farm, used as the cemetery chapel, was probably re-built in 1778 but a window in the malmstone part has the style of 1330. It may be the royal chapel documented in 1362.

Kingsley Mill stands on the Kingsley Stream at its confluence with the Oakhanger Stream to form the Oxney Stream (River Slea). The mill in brick and cottage in malmstone and ironstone form a single building. The two wheels have gone but most of the mechanism is still intact, all timber. It had four pairs of stones. Milling ceased in 1916 and it is now a private residence.

Lasham was ESSEHĀ in the Domesday Book, a manor in Odiham Hundred. It was part of the demesne of the king but had been held in freehold by one Hakon before the Conquest. The church, St Mary, is Victorian but is on the site of earlier churches. It was built in 1866 in Early English style with a single lancet as the east window. The list of Rectors starts before 1284.

Lasham Airfield is much in evidence because of its gliders but being on high ground is not often seen. It is the maintenance HQ of several small air travel companies. It was built in World War II, bombed before completion in 1942, and used mainly by fighters and fighter bombers cooperating with the army in tank busting and road and rail disruption. Later in the war, attacks were made on V2 launch ramps and other precision targets, including a Gestapo records office. Canadian, Netherlands and Polish squadrons operated here.

Lavant is a local name for temporary streams which rise after much rain.

Lynchets are steps in ground level, sometimes indicating pre-historic farming. Soil creep down to a hedge, and away from it below, left the step when the hedge was removed. Large ancient lynchets may have belts of trees. Lynchets occur in woods and towns. Strip lynchets are narrow fields like terraces.

Malmscarp - malmstone escarpment - see box page 45

Medstead has a small earthen fort, possibly Iron Age. The name, *Medested* first appears in 1202 but places in a 701 charter of King Ine, suggest it was part of the 40 mansae (hides) of Alresford granted by King Cenwealh 643-672, to the church of Winchester. It is not mentioned in the Domesday Book being then taxed as part of Alresford. The first known non-ecclesiastical lord of the manor was Richard Houtot in 1346. The church, St Andrew, dates from about 1160 but is almost certainly the successor to one of the three Domesday Book churches of Alresford suggesting the village already existed then. Though modernized and lengthened in 1833, it still has Norman arches.

The **Meon Valley** line was a branch of the LSWR (London & SW Railway Co) from Alton to Fareham where it joined the Eastleigh-Gosport line. It opened in 1903, ceased carrying passengers in 1955 and closed in 1968.

Mill Court has a small estate on both sides of the river. It was a manor by 1367 but is not in the Domesday Book. The main house is built of malmstone. The oast houses and barn have been converted to residences.

Monk Wood caps a chalk hillock. It has complex medieval mounds linked to the Waverley monks for whom the Neatham land was a grange.

Monty, Field Marshal Montgomery, 1887-1976, lived in retirement at Isington Mill and lies in Binsted churchyard. He was the best known British soldier of World War II. His defeat of the German and Italian armies at Alamein in North Africa was the turning point for the western war as a whole and he went on to take charge of the D-Day invasion over the beaches of Normandy, then to command the British and Canadian armies in Europe.

Neatham is now a small cluster of houses but was a large Saxon royal manor, HQ of Neatham Hundred and reached to Alice Holt. Domesday Book NETEHĀ had land for 52 ploughs, 8½ mills and a market. In 1147 King Stephen gave it to Waverley Abbey and it was tilled by the monks. The manor house is an 18th century red brick building around an Elizabethan core. Lower Neatham Mill functioned until 1962 and is probably on one of the Domesday Book mill sites.

Newton Valence, NEWENTONE in the Domesday Book had a mill, a church and 100 pigsworth of woodland. In 1249 Henry III gave the manor to his Poitou half-brother William de Valence who also acquired the heiress and title of the Earl of Pembroke. Aylmer, his 23 year old brother was elected Bishop by the Winchester monks under duress in 1250. French relatives were one cause of the unrest at the time of Henry III which led to the Barons' Revolt associated with Simon de Montfort, castellan of Odiham. The present church dates from about 1220. The lancets of the east end are of the Early English style that preceded a single large east window. The tower was added in the 15th century.

Noar Hill is a chalk hill with High Wood Hanger on the north face and Noar Hill Hanger on the south. Flints are not much in evidence for it has been denuded of the Upper Chalk which has most flints. It is a watershed: the spring on the north side becomes the Oakhanger Stream flowing via the River Wey to the Thames and one on the south side becomes the River Rother, draining via the Arun to the English Channel. Hill names like Noar, Nower and Nor derive from the Saxon *ōra* with *n* from a preceding word eg *atten*. There were numerous differentiating words for hills as people lived out of doors and needed aids to navigation. Fieldwork on hills of similar name suggests an *ōra* was a hill with a flat top and a convex side. Margaret Gelling & Ann Cole *Landscape of Place-names* 2000

Oakhanger is the Domesday Book manor of ACANGRE which was broken up between several owners in early times. James of Oakhanger, who gave some of the land for building Selborne Priory, had amongst his feudal duties to supply one foot soldier for 40 days p.a. and to maintain the bridge over the stream, commemorated in the name of the nearby cottage, Tunbridge. The church, St Mary Magdalen, is Victorian (1868). The medieval church, a chapel of ease of Selborne, was on the south side of the Oakhanger Stream near Chapel Farm which may have been the village centre at that time.

Oakhanger - the story of a Hampshire Village Jean Chapple 1986 Paul Cave 88pp

The **oil gathering station** of the Humbly Grove Oil Field is well concealed by earth banks and forest. The initial exploratory well was sunk in 1980 and the site has operated since 1986. In 2005 it was equipped to use the depleted oil bearing rocks as a reservoir for imported gas. Huge compressors were built for the quantity and forces involved. Horizontal drill holes had to be made into the reservoir rock. The outgoing gas is cleaned and regulated to 55 bar. By 2012, 6m barrels of oil and 49½m cubic feet of native gas had been extracted. The new stored gas forces up more oil and it is estimated 70,000 more barrels may be collected over 7 years. Oil is piped in as a hot mixture of salt water and gas from several well-heads in the surrounding country. The liquid is further heated to keep the tars and waxes mobile, and allowed to stand for the water to settle out below the oil. The oil is piped to a railhead near Holybourne on the A31. The water is pumped back down to force up more oil. Stored gas arrives and leaves by a 24" pipe linked to the national network. The reservoir rocks at 4000 feet and 5000 feet hold 10 bcf (billion cubic feet), compressed more than 100 times at 110 bar and 145 bar. The reserve is about, $\frac{1}{40}$ of an average day's supply for the country. This reservoir is particularly useful for rapid gas trading and for fluctuating demand because it can store and output gas faster than others. Imported gas comes by pipe from Norway and Russia and by tanker from the Gulf states and Egypt. Quantities are monitored by National Grid.

Data Courtesy of Humbly Grove Energy

Two **oil pipelines** with ESSO marker posts pass under the area. Built in the 1960s, they run from the refinery at Fawley and branch near Alton to Heathrow and Gatwick. The 10 inch pipe carries only aviation fuel. The 12 inch pipe carries different products at different times for distribution in the London area.

The **oil terminal** beside the A31 is where the pipeline from the Humbly Grove oil wells, 3 miles to the north, meets the railway.

Parks were originally for keeping deer. They required the king's license so are usually datable, mostly medieval. A park pale, if visible, is a linear mound which, when new, would have been higher with tall wooden palings to contain the deer. A rich landowner might convert part of one of his manors into a park including his house, which also became known as the Park. Publicly funded civic parks commenced with Birkenhead Park which opened in 1847.

Pax Hill was the home of Lord Baden Powell from 1918 to 1938. The house had been built in 1907 but B-P changed its name to celebrate the ending of the Great War. It has since been a school and nursing home.

Preston Candover is a linear village in rolling chalkland. Candefer in Alfred the Great's will was a bequest to his daughter. CANDOVRE in the Domesday Book was the address of eight manors. Three of these correspond to Brown Candover, Chilton Candover and Moundsmere but the others cannot be distinguished. They belonged to Ralph de Mortimer, Hugh de Port, Cheping two clerks and Edwin the priest. One had a 19th century Lord of the Manor called Purefoys. The church, St Mary, Victorian Gothic, was built in 1884 in brick with flint facings. The elegant shingled spire interests woodpeckers. The previous church, built around 1170, still exists at the other end of the village. The priest listed in the Domesday Book suggests there was a church in 1086; his rectory may have been the original Preston (priest's farm).

Priors Dean village consists of a Norman church and two houses. King John added the estate to the adjacent Colemore which belonged to Southwick Priory (near Porchester). They became part of the Titchborne Inheritance. Manor Farmhouse is 17th century with a 3-storey brick front.

Priors Dean Vineyard is at 500 feet. It was not planted until 1988. Bacchus, Angevine and Seyval Blanc are grown in alternate rows to make fine white wine. The vines are high trained. To visit phone 01730 894147 or use website.

Priory Farm conceals the remnants of Selborne Priory but its plan can be surmised from digs and by analogy with other Augustinian Priories. It was founded in 1232 by Peter des Roches, a military knight whom King John made Bishop of Winchester and guardian to the child Henry III who lived at Guildford. The prior led 12 canons who prayed like monks but also preached. The initial endowment was a site bought from James of Oakhanger but many gifts followed and most of the Manor of Selborne came into the priory's ownership. Churches, town houses and land followed so by 1348 it had more than 2000 acres, some leased and some cultivated by its own workers. William of Wyckham, as Bishop of Winchester, inspected the priory and told the canons *inter alia* to take lessons in the scriptures, avoid luxury clothes and sleep with their drawers on. After 250 years the priory was in decline and Magdalen College, founded by Bishop Waynflete of Winchester, asked for its closure and its property, confirmed by papal bull in 1486. Thus it avoided Dissolution and its documents survived but the stone was removed for building elsewhere.

Selborne Priory E M Yates 1995 25pp

The **pumping station** at Oakhanger supplies the surrounding villages with 1m gallons of water a day from a 100m borehole in the Lower Greensand, whose lowest stratum is the impervious Atherfield Clay. Filtration and chlorination are carried out at the cunningly unobtrusive cottage-like building built about 1978.

The **radomes** at Oakhanger are fibre glass covers protecting large parabolic antennae (dish aerials) for satellite control at military and civil stations in Oakhanger village and the nearby Slab Common. The War Department bought the land in 1938 for wireless stations; the bowl-shaped terrain makes it electrically-quiet. The RAF formed 1001 Signals Unit in 1968 to run the Skynet terminal in Oakhanger. The site near the village is American and the Slab Common sites are now run by civilian companies. The stations receive from military and civilian satellites and control their positions and use.

Rhode was LARODE in the Domesday Book, a small manor in Neatham Hundred owned by Geoffrey the Chamberlain, rated at 1 hide + 1 virgate but tax-free. Briogic had been the owner before the Conquest.

The **Roman Pottery** at Alice Holt mass-produced pots and tiles for 400 years from about AD 70. Alice Holt Ware is found at digs all over southern England and, rarely, in Northern France. The site came to light when the Portsmouth turnpike was built in the 1870s, cutting through acres of broken pots in spoil heaps. The underlying Gault clay, peat turf for kiln building and abundant wood made the area suitable, probably already used by Iron Age potters. Kilns of the first century were stacks of pots packed with wood and covered by turfs, 1½m in diameter, surrounded by C-shaped mounds of spoil. Only their bases can be detected; later kilns had stone walls. Experimental archæology suggests the best fuel was straight branches of 60cm, 5cm thick; coppicing was probably already in use. *The Alice Holt/Farnham Pottery Industry* M A B Lyne & R S Jeffries 1979 77pp

The **Roman road** was a link between the (tribal) district capitals Calleva Atrebatum (Silchester) and Noviomagus Regnensium (Chichester), crossing the Wey at the putative Vindomis (Neatham/Holybourne). It was first spotted in aerial survey photographs in 1949 but has now been traced on the ground for most of its route. Rarely is it followed by modern roads or tracks probably because Calleva Atrebatum was abandoned at the end of the Roman period.

Ropley is a village of ancient houses and lanes on a ridge of the Upper Chalk which is responsible for the flints in the fields and the buildings. The name may derive from *Hroppa's Clearing* when the area was much more forested. The land was part of the Bishop of Winchester's manor of Bishop's Sutton in the Domesday Book and does not appear as a separate manor until around 1310. William of Wykeham used the land to endow Winchester College in 1390. The Church, St Peter, is presumably on the site of a chapel recorded in 1241. It was rebuilt in Victorian times but still has a 13th century door in the flint walls.

The River **Rother** flows near Petersfield and Midhurst to join the Arun at Pulborough, draining to the English Channel.

St Catherine's Hill is the property of Winchester College but is managed by Hampshire Wildlife Trust. It has a rich chalk grassland flora and fauna. There is evidence of Bronze Age habitation and the ring mound is Iron Age fortification. The mizmaze, on top, is a pattern cut out of the turf. Its origin is obscure but there is no reference to it earlier than late 17th century. Tradition has it that a College boy dug it during a vacation when he was not allowed to leave. On the south side are Plague Pits, mass graves from the Black Death. There was a 12th century chapel on top that was in use until Tudor times.

St Cross Hospital (01962 878218 & website) is open to the public most of the year. The fine medieval buildings are almshouses with church. The master's house is outside the main gate. The 17 brothers of the original foundation wear a black gown with a silver cross; 8 brothers of the Order of Noble Poverty wear a red gown with cardinal's badge. St Cross is the oldest charity in Britain. Henry de Blois, 3rd Norman Bishop of Winchester (half brother of King Stephen) founded it circa 1135 for *thirteen poor men, feeble and so reduced in strength that they can scarcely or not at all support themselves ....*

Selborne was brought to the attention of the world by Gilbert White. It is an excellent centre for walking and an attractive village with many thatched and malmstone houses. Fisher Lodge was the poorhouse from 1780-1835 and was attacked during the tithe riots of 1830. Sir Adam de Gurdon may have owned the 6½' skeleton found under the church. He gave the Plestor to the village, the play area or fairground in front of the churchyard. Selborne has two entries in the Domesday Book as SELESBVRNE and LESBORNE. Later in the middle ages the Priory became effectively Lord of the Manor, followed by Magdalen College which acquired the Priory.

Selborne Church, Saint Mary, is Saxon in foundation but the building dates from about 1180. Points of interest: fluted capitals of the pillars typical of Norman churches in the area; arches pointed but unadorned, transitional between round Norman and moulded Gothic: 13th century oak door and ironwork; primitive font, possibly Saxon; oak beam over the organ, 1910; king post roof, 1883; clock mechanism; Gilbert White's grave outside the NE corner. The Gilbert White on the black stone by the altar was his grandfather.

Shalden was SELDENE in the Domesday Book, a manor in the Hundred of Odiham belonging to William Mauduit. The church, SS Peter & Paul, was built in 1863 in plain 13th century style on the site of an earlier church whose 15th century font is still in use. John Lightfoot, the botanist, was Rector 1765-77.

Telegraph House, built 1828, was to have been a semaphore station in the chain from the Admiralty to Plymouth but its mast and signalling arms were not installed. The Portsmouth chain operated from 1822 but work on the Plymouth branch from Chatley Heath stopped in 1831 when electric telegraph was mooted. The adjacent stations were at the Hog's Back Hotel and Four Marks.

Temple Manor takes its name from a Knights Templar preceptory known to be here in 1240. The Templars sold part of the small estate to Selborne Priory in 1250 to raise £200 for purchases in the Holy Land. There is a tradition, started by Gilbert White on slender evidence, that Adam de Gurdon lived here on a small estate possibly bequeathed to the Templars.

Thedden appears from a fine of 1203 to have been a medieval manor. It was given to Selborne Priory. The Georgian house dates from 1810.

Twyford Down figures in the annals of road construction protests. The first part of the M3 opened in 1971 but the section in the cutting was not completed until 1995. Disruption of enquiries and obstruction of the building caused multiple delays. Three ways around Winchester were considered: a tunnel, a cutting or a widening of the 1930s by-pass at the water meadows. This by-pass between St Catherine's Hill and the railway next to the Navigation has been obliterated.

Hawkley **Warren Nature Reserve** is owned by Hampshire County Council. It is beech woodland on the precipitous sides of a chalk combe with rare orchids.

Well is a hamlet surrounded by arable country. It was an estate cut out of Long Sutton Manor in the 12th century. The road through it on the ridge is the Harow Way, the prehistoric route from Cornwall to Kent called Pilgrims' Way in Surrey. It is said to be the Tin Road but no ingots have been found associated with it. The name may derive from *hoar*, old, or *herge*, temple; it passes Stonehenge.

West Court was a manor sold from Binsted in 1333 to finance a chaplain for the church. The house has timbers dated to 1314. Richard de Westcote, whose stone effigy is in the church, was the purchaser.

Weston Common is managed by the Forestry Commission. There is no felling plan for most of the broad-leaved trees; they re-seed themselves. Southern beech and Norway maple have been planted at the eastern edge. The conifers are for felling after 60 years. Commercial conifers do not grow well on chalk, apart from Western Hemlock, but here the clay-with-flints layer and Ice age deposits over the chalk are sufficiently thick to sustain the trees.

River **Wey** is the name of two local rivers. One starts at Alton, flows between Binsted and Froyle, past Farnham and Waverley Abbey. The other Wey rises at Waggoners' Wells and collects Selborne brooks via the Oakhanger Stream and River Slea. These Weys are considered to have been tributaries of the Blackwater River captured during the Ice Age by the main Wey which they join at Tilford. That flows through Guildford to the Thames at Weybridge.

Wick Hill Farm was the domicile of Farmer Tull mentioned by Gilbert White. It is recorded as early as 1250 when a Will de Wyke is listed. The trig point was built in January 1937 (for £5 15s 6d) at the start of the third triangulation of Great Britain - a secondary point. Most trig points are now redundant but a few are used as reference points for GPS or maintained to give joy to walkers.

Wield was WALDE in the Domesday Book, a large manor of 10 hides held after the Conquest by Durand from the Bishop of Winchester. A mill recorded in 1286, was probably a windmill, for the land reaches 576 feet. Upper Wield village looks ancient because of its nucleus of thatched cottages and Norman church, St James, which dates from about 1150. Points of interest: small Norman rounded chancel and door arches; large squints beside the chancel arch; gallery; traces of early paintings on the nave walls; splendid alabaster carving of William Waloppe (died 1617) and wife; unusual (modern) colouring of the ceiling. The nave and chancel appear to be of the same age.

William of Wykeham, 1324-1410, was Bishop of Winchester and founder of Winchester College. An ordinary boy-made-good, he was born at Wickham near Fareham and sent to grammar school in Winchester probably by his Lord of the Manor. He became, in turn, secretary at Winchester Castle, clerk of works of Windsor Castle, Warden of the Royal Forests and Keeper of the Privy Seal. Church posts provided his income. He did not enter holy orders until 1361 but was Bishop by1366 and Chancellor of England by 1368. Edward III blamed him for territorial losses in France and he resigned as chancellor. While under a cloud he lived at the abbeys of Merton, Newark, Woking and Waverley. On Richard II's accession the charges against him were overturned and he reluctantly returned to the chancellorship. Although his great wealth came from pluralism he spent it in good works, founding and funding New College Oxford and Winchester College and rebuilding much of the cathedral.

Winchester has a tourist office (01962 840500) which provides daily guided tours. Now the County Town of Hampshire, its claim to be the ancient capital of England stems from Egbert, king of Wessex, 802-839 (grandfather of Alfred the Great and 34th great grandfather of Elizabeth II). He became bretwalda around 830 and founded the dynasty that would unite the Saxon and Danish kingdoms that became England. The tax rating of 1086, satirically known as Domesday Book, was, politely, LIBER DE WINTONIA. The English Treasury remained in Winchester until the 13th century

There was a pre-historic population but the many layers of building confuse archæological investigation. Belgic tribes migrated here around 50BC. The Romans called it Venta Belgarum and built the town wall around 200AD. Alfred the Great made it a burh. The town had a mayor and grammar school in the time of King John (1200) but was not a corporation until 1327. Plagues, Dissolution of the Monasteries and the Civil War caused three centuries of decay. In the Civil War, Winchester was captured by Sir William Waller, re-captured for the king then bombarded by Cromwell. After the Restoration Wren began a 150-room palace for Charles II but it was never completed. The Industrial Revolution passed Winchester by and it became a city of shopkeepers and the professions. By 1850 it was a tourist attraction.

Winchester Cathedral was started by Bishop Walkelin in 1079. The transepts are Walkelin's but much of the rest has been replaced in later medieval styles. The original tower crashed down on William Rufus' tomb in 1107. The oak choir stalls date from 1308.   Queen Mary was married to Philip of Spain here in 1554. Built on peat it has had to be underpinned under water by a diver, 1906-11. The medieval See was the richest in land ownership after Milan.

The Roman missionary to the West Saxons, Birinus who arrived in 664, settled at Dorchester on Thames. A later bishop, Hædda, moved to Winchester in 675 when King Cenwealh built a church. It was just north of the present cathedral and became Oldminster. Alfred the Great's Queen founded Nunnaminster (near the Guildhall) and their son, Edward the Elder, built Newminster on the land of Old Minster. Bishop Ethelwold made the minsters abbeys in 963. Oldminster became St Swithun's Abbey, a great centre of learning, famous for illuminated manuscripts. Nunnaminster became St Mary's Abbey. Newminster became Hyde Abbey. At Dissolution the buildings were quarried for their stone. The Prior & Convent of St Swithun became the Dean & Chapter of the Cathedral.

Winchester College has about 700 boys. There is no uniform but the scholars wear gowns. Alumni are Wykehamists. Founded by William of Wykeham in 1387 and opened in 1394, most of its original buildings still serve their original purposes. It was for 70 scholars, including 10 commoners, "sons of noble or powerful people". Its novelty was being set up as an independent corporation which took commoners. This made it the model for Eton and the later English Public Schools. At the Dissolution, it survived when church-funded schools were closed, helped by a gift of a silver plate to Thomas Cromwell. It also survived the Commonwealth; influential Parliamentarians were Wykehamists.

Wivelrod, a hamlet of Bentworth, was sold as a manor in 1259. Edward Knight, Jane Austen's brother, inherited it with Chawton and sold it in 1840.

Wolvesey Palace may be visited by the public (01962 854766), Apr-Sept. The fortified part is now a ruin but the living quarters remain as the bishop's palace. The Bishop of Winchester owned five castles.

East **Worldham** was an agricultural village, a cluster of large farmhouses with cottages between and modern infill. It was WERILDEHĀ in the Domesday Book, a small holding of 5 virgates in the large Royal Hundred of Neatham held after the Conquest by Geoffrey the Marshall. The Roman house under the churchyard and the nearby Celtic open field patterns make plausible continuity in estates from pre-Roman time through the Dark Ages and until the manor was broken up in 1963. Robert de Venuz, probably the son or grandson of William the Marshall, is documented in 1197 paying the fine to inherit the manor. This makes him the first known keeper of Alice Holt and Woolmer Forest - a post linked to the Lordship. The church, St Mary, dates from around 1180 but was substantially rebuilt in 1865. The advowson was gifted to Selborne Priory in 1254 and passed with the priory's property to Magdalen College in 1418. Points of interest: the original apse arch, external in the east wall; modern lancets; a carved effigy, possibly Geoffrey Chaucer's widow Phillipa; their son Thomas was Lord of the Manor 1412-34.

West **Worldham** is not listed in the Domesday Book but was probably hived off in the 12th century as the endowment for the church. It was re-united with East Worldham around 1500. "Worldham Minor" had *domicilia tenentes* X in 1428, about the same as now. Hammonds Farm was the manor house. The 12th century church, St Nicholas, was endowed by Richard de Annecy as chapel of ease to Hamble Priory, a cell of the Benedictine Abbey of Tiron (near Chartres). William of Wykeham bought its estate for Winchester College which is still responsible for the chancel. Points of interest; original doorway; east window renewed at the time of WofW's purchase; 15th century porch.

Wyck, a hamlet of Binsted parish, has a rectangle of roads characteristic of settlements overlying Roman villas; so far, only the bath house has been excavated. Wyck Place, a 17th century mansion with Victorian additions, was the seat of the Wyckhams and the Bonham-Carters for 300 years up to 1994.